Practice Book

NATIONAL GEOGRAPHIC

Reach™

Language • Literacy • Content

NATIONAL GEOGRAPHIC   Hampton-Brown

Acknowledgments and credits continue on the inside back cover.
National Geographic and the Yellow Border are registered trademarks of the National Geographic Society.

National Geographic School Publishing
Hampton-Brown
www.NGSP.com

Printed in the USA.
DB Hess, Woodstock, IL

ISBN: 978-0-7362-7465-4

13 14 15 16 17 18 19   10 9 8 7 6 5 4 3

HPS230091

Contents

Unit 1: Crossing Between Cultures

Unit 2: Catching the Light

Unit 3: Nature's Network

Unit 4: Justice

Unit 5: Every Drop

Unit 6: The Wild West

Unit 7: Moving Through Space

Unit 8: One Idea

Name _____   Date _____

Crossing Between Cultures

**Make a concept map with the answers to the Big Question:
How can where you are change who you are?**

How can where you are change who you are?

1.1

© P/HB

Name _____   Date _____

How a Character Changes

Beginning	Middle	End

P & HB

© **Use this chart to tell about a partner's favorite story. How does the character feel at first? How do the character's feelings change?**

Name _____   Date _____

A New Sport

Grammar Rules Complete Subject and Predicate

1. The complete subject includes all the words in the subject.
2. The complete predicate includes all the words in the predicate.

Underline the complete subject. Circle the complete predicate.

1. My family and I moved to the United States.

2. We stayed with my aunt and uncle.

3. A boy named Mike lived next door.

4. Mike and his friends taught me how to play basketball.

5. Now basketball is one of my favorite sports.

Write a sentence about a culture you know and read it to a partner. Have your partner name the complete subject and complete predicate.

P/HB

©

Name _____   Date _____

My Diary from Here to There

Amada learns her family is moving from Mexico to the United States. She is scared to leave her country and her friends. Even though there will be many opportunities in California, Amada is worried she won't learn English. Her father tells her she is stronger than she thinks.

Amada and her family leave for her grandparents' home on the border. When her father goes to Los Angeles, her family tries to make her laugh. Finally, her father sends green cards and they can cross the border. Her grandmother gives her a journal and tells her to keep her culture and language alive in her diary and her heart.

They meet Papá at a bus station in Los Angeles. She realizes that even though she is far away from her country, friends, and family, it doesn't mean they are not with her. They are in her diary and her language. Papá was right—she is stronger than she thought.

© P/HB

Grammar: Simple Subject and Predicate

Find Those Parts!

Grammar Rules Simple Subject and Predicate

1. The simple subject is the most important word in the complete subject.
2. The simple predicate is the verb.

Work with a team of four.

1. The first person underlines the simple subject.

My older brother likes spaghetti with tomato sauce.

2. The second person circles the complete subject.

My older brother likes spaghetti with tomato sauce.

3. The third person draws a star over the simple predicate.

My older brother likes spaghetti with tomato sauce.

4. The fourth person draws two lines under the complete

predicate.

My older brother likes spaghetti with tomato sauce.

Now try it with these sentences.

- Our grandmother cooks the best rice and tofu dishes.
- My friends want hot dogs.
- Our uncle misses the bread from his town in Italy.

© P/HB

Name _____   Date _____

Vocabulary Bingo

1. **Write one Key Word in each square.**

2. **Listen to the clues. Find the Key Word and use a marker to cover it.**

3. **Say "Bingo" when you have four markers in a row.**

1.6

P/HB
©

Name _____ Date _____

My Diary from Here to There

Beginning	Middle	End

Use this chart to tell about Amada's story. Then use your character development chart to retell the story to a partner.

P/HB ©

Name _____   Date _____

My Diary from Here to There

Expression in reading is how you use your voice to express feeling. Use this passage to practice reading with proper expression.

Today at breakfast, Mamá explained everything. She said, "Papá lost his job.	12
There's no work here, no jobs at all. We know moving will be hard, but we want	29
the best for all of you. Try to understand." I thought the boys would be upset, but	46
instead they got really excited about moving to the States.	56
Am I the only one who is scared of leaving our home, our beautiful country,	71
and all the people we might never see again?	80

From "My Diary from Here to There" page 14

Expression

B ☐ Does not read with feeling.   A ☐ Reads with appropriate feeling for most content.

I ☐ Reads with some feeling, but does not match content.   AH ☐ Reads with appropriate feeling for all content.

Accuracy and Rate Formula

Use the formula to measure a reader's accuracy and rate while reading aloud.

_____	−	_____	=	_____
words attempted in one minute		number of errors		words correct per minute (wcpm)

P/HB

©

Name _____ Date _____

Complete this chart as you read the oral history.

Page	My Question	The Answer

P/HB

🗨 **Tell a partner one of your questions. Then try to answer your partner's question.**

Respond and Extend: Venn Diagram

Compare Genres

Compare fiction and nonfiction.

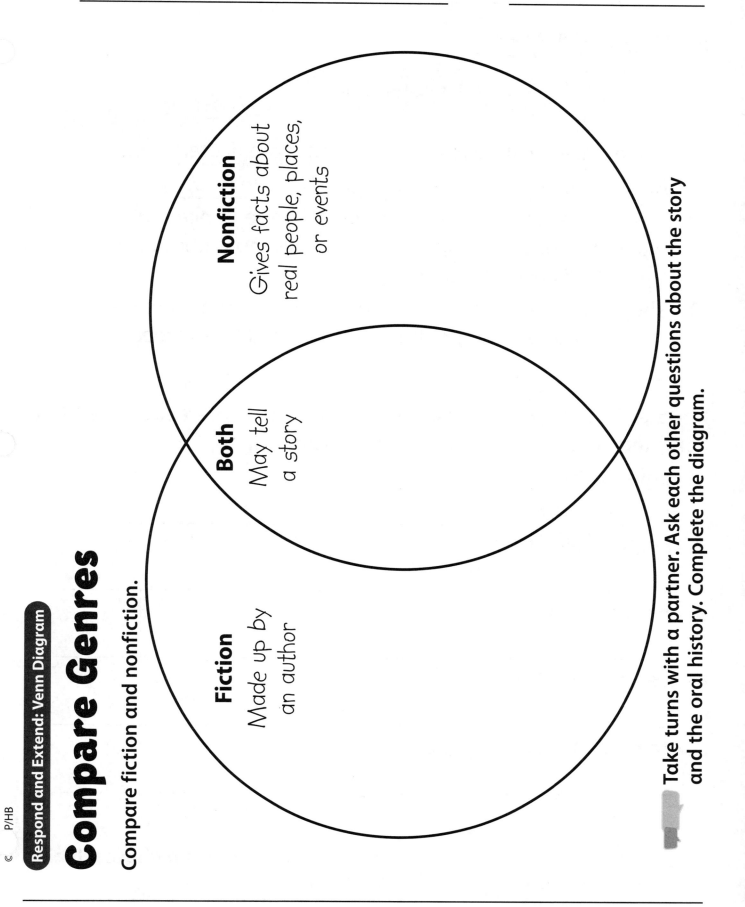

Nonfiction

Gives facts about real people, places, or events

Both

May tell a story

Fiction

Made up by an author

Take turns with a partner. Ask each other questions about the story and the oral history. Complete the diagram.

Grammar: Complete Sentences

Grammar Rules Complete Sentences

1. A sentence must have a <u>subject</u> and a <u>predicate.</u>
   <u>*His favorite grandmother*</u> <u>*makes good Korean food.*</u>

2. The simple subject is what or whom the sentence is about: *grandmother.* The complete subject tells more about that subject: *His favorite grandmother.*

3. The simple predicate is the verb: *makes.* The complete predicate tells more about the predicate: *makes good Korean food.*

Read each group of words. Add a subject or a predicate to write a complete sentence. Use correct punctuation.

1. came to visit

   She came to visit.
   _____

2. Greg's whole family

   _____

3. entered the harbor

   _____

4. everyone on shore

   _____

5. ate Korean food for dinner

   _____

 Work with a partner. Pick one group of words from above. Think of as many complete sentences as you can.

Thinking Map: Venn Diagram

Map and Talk

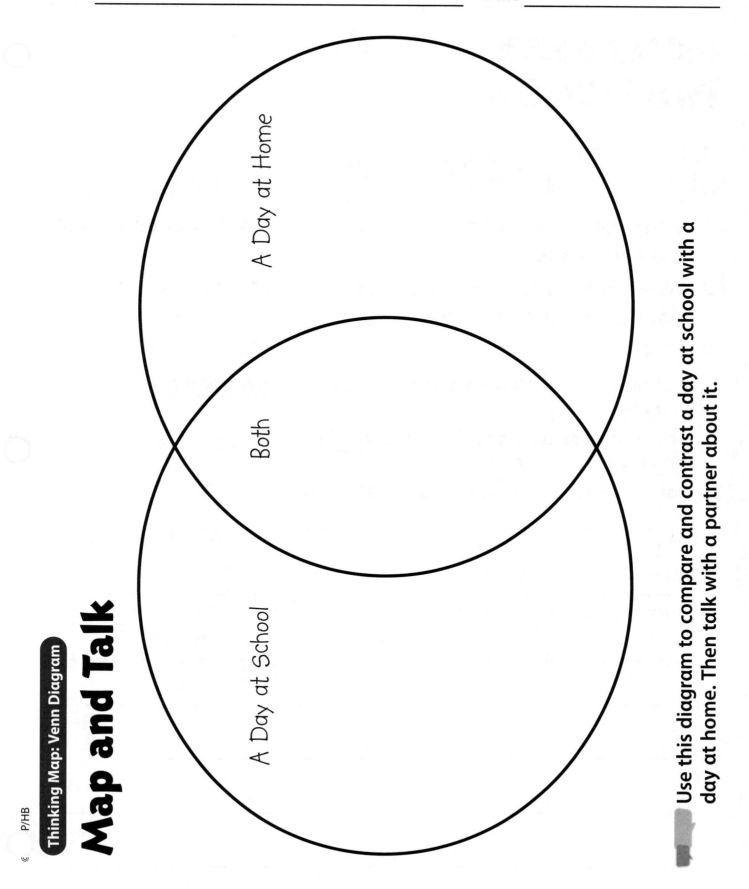

A Day at Home

Both

A Day at School

Use this diagram to compare and contrast a day at school with a day at home. Then talk with a partner about it.

Grammar: Compound Subject

Two into One

Grammar Rules Compound Subjects

1. When **and** joins two simple subjects, use a verb that tells about more than one.

2. When **or** joins two subjects, use a verb that agrees with the simple subject closest to it.

1. **Find sentences with the same <u>predicate</u>. Jen <u>bakes bread</u>. Ed <u>bakes bread</u>.**

2. **Write a new sentence with a <u>compound</u> <u>subject</u>. <u>Jen and Ed</u> bake bread.**

3. **Make sure your new subject agrees with the verb.**

Tim makes great tacos.	Bill makes great tacos.	Lan arrives at the party first.	My mother cooks family dinners.
Jimmy buys spices at the store.	My father cooks family dinners.	Lin buys spices at the store.	Sara arrives at the party first.

_____

_____

_____

_____

Name _____   Date _____

The Autobiography of John Bul Dau

1

John Bul Dau lived in a village in Sudan. His early life was very happy. One night, his village was attacked by soldiers. John hid and escaped. For four months he and a neighbor walked towards a refugee camp in Ethiopia. They stayed there for four years.

2

A civil war in Ethiopia forced John to walk 500 miles to a refugee camp in Kenya with many other Sudanese boys, or Lost Boys. In the camp he started first grade. He was 18 years old. He studied hard and soon he graduated from high school.

3

In 2001, John moved to Syracuse, New York. He found a job and started college. He began several organizations to help other Lost Boys in the United States and around the world. He is no longer lost!

iP & HB

Grammar: Compound Predicates

The Lost Boys

Grammar Rules Compound Predicates

A compound predicate has two or more verbs joined by **and** or **or**.

Combine the sentences to write one longer sentence.

1. Many Lost Boys were orphaned. Many Lost Boys were separated from their families.

   _____

2. The boys escaped from soldiers. The boys traveled for many miles.

   _____

   _____

3. They lived in different places. They walked to different countries.

   _____

4. The boys went to refugee camps. The boys got an education.

   _____

5. Students stayed in Kakuma. Students moved to the United States.

   _____

   _____

Write two sentences with the same subject. Use a different verb in each sentence. Have a partner combine the sentences into one sentence that has a compound predicate.

© P/HB

Vocabulary: Apply Word Knowledge

Words Around the World

1. The traveler stands behind a challenger.

2. Listen to the definition. Find the Key Word and call it out.

3. The first to answer correctly travels to the next student. The first traveler to go all around the circle wins.

KEY WORDS

citizenship	customs	identity	adapt	origin

DEFINITIONS:

• where you come from

• who you are

• traditions

• being a citizen

• to change

P & HB

A Refugee Remembers

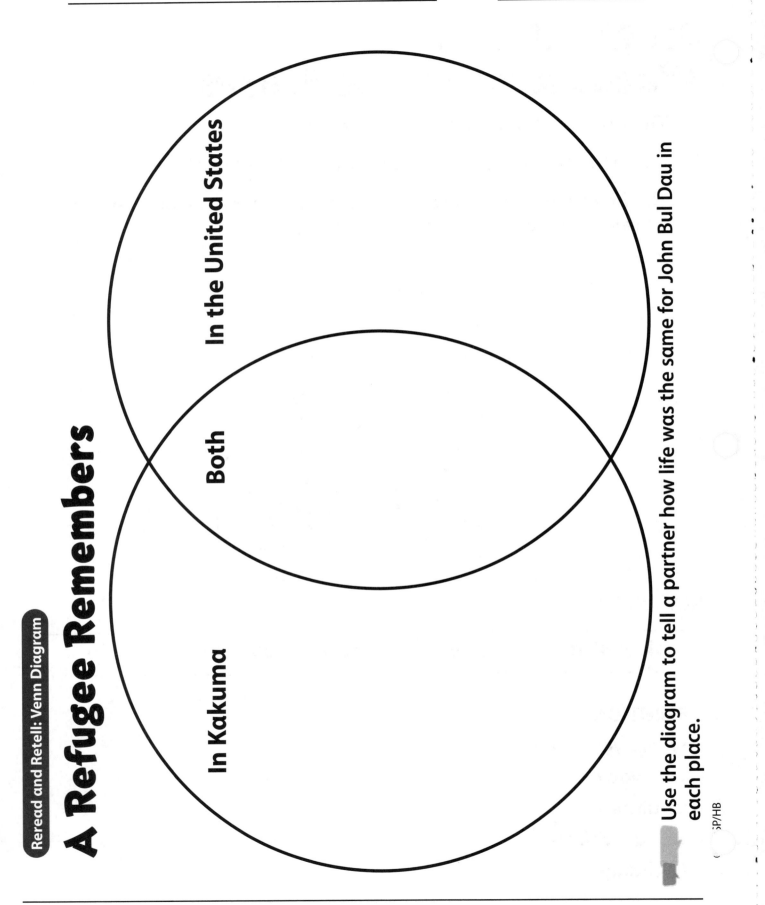

In the United States

Both

In Kakuma

Use the diagram to tell a partner how life was the same for John Bul Dau in each place.

SP/HB

Fluency: Expression

A Refugee Remembers

Expression is when you show feeling in your voice as you read. Use this passage from p. 49 to practice reading with proper expression. Look for words and punctuation marks that tell you about the mood or feeling of what you are reading.

All that night, as we waited in the grass for	10
death or daybreak, I thought the man who pulled me	20
to safety was my father. When the sun began to rise,	31
I learned I was wrong. Abraham Deng Niop was	40
my neighbor.	42
After about two hours the guns fell silent and we	52
heard no more sounds from the village. Abraham told	61
me we ought to move.	66
Every time we heard noises coming toward us,	74
we ducked into the forest or the tall grass. Soldiers kept	85
passing. When they disappeared, we started running again.	93
East seemed a good direction; we heard no guns as we	104
ran toward the rising sun.	109

Expression

B ☐ Does not read with feeling. **A** ☐ Reads with appropriate feeling for most content.

I ☐ Reads with some feeling, but does not match content. **AH** ☐ Reads with appropriate feeling for all content.

Accuracy and Rate Formula

Use the formula to measure a reader's accuracy and rate while reading aloud.

_____ − _____ = _____

words attempted   number of errors   words correct per minute
in one minute   (wcpm)

Name _____ Date _____

Dialogue Journal

What I think	What do you think?
Page _____ _____ _____ _____	_____ _____ _____ _____
Page _____ _____ _____ _____	_____ _____ _____ _____
Page _____ _____ _____ _____	_____ _____ _____ _____
Page _____ _____ _____ _____	_____ _____ _____ _____

Tell a partner your thoughts about each page. Then ask your partner to share his or her thoughts.

P/HB

©

Compare Literary Language

John Bul Dau	Students in "American Stories"

P & HB

©

🔲 **Take turns with a partner. Compare the literary language used in both selections.**

Name _____   Date _____

Grammar: Compound Subjects and Subject-Verb Agreement

Grammar Rules Compound Subjects

1. When **and** joins two simple subjects, use a verb that tells about more than one.

2. When **or** joins two subjects, use a verb that agrees with the simple subject closest to it.

Read each pair of sentences. Combine the subjects into a compound subject and write the new sentence. Be sure your subject agrees with the verb.

1. Mom goes to the city. Dad goes to the city.

_____

2. The train brings them downtown. The bus brings them downtown.

_____

3. The grocery store is open. The bakery is open.

_____

4. The vegetables are fresh. The bread is fresh.

_____

Make two sentences with the same subjects. Have your partner combine them into one sentence with a compound subject.

Focus and Coherence

	Is the main idea focus clear?	**Does the writing feel complete? Do the ideas fit together well?**
4 Wow!	• The main idea is clear. • All the details and examples are about the main idea.	• The writing feels complete. • The topic sentence and the ending sentence go together well.
3 Ahh.	• The main idea is fairly clear. • Most of the details and examples are about the main idea.	• The writing feels mostly complete. • The topic sentence and the ending sentence could be a better fit.
2 Hmm.	• The main idea is not very clear. • Few of the details and examples are about the main idea.	• The writing could be more complete. • The topic sentence and the ending sentence do not fit together well.
1 Huh?	• The main idea is difficult to understand. • The details and examples are not about the main idea.	• The writing is not complete. • The topic sentence and the ending sentence do not fit together.

Name _____ Date _____

T-Chart

Write your topic. Then write details in the chart about a time you had to adjust to a new situation or place.

Central Topic: _____

Setting 1: _____	**Setting 2:** _____

© :P & HB

Writing Project: Revise

Revise

Use the Revising Marks to revise this paragraph. Revise for:

- **relevant details**
- **concluding sentence.**

Revising Marks	
∧	Add.
℘	Delete.
⌐	Indent.

The plaza in my town in mexico has many food sellers.

There are mountains nearby. Farmers cell fruit and vegetables. Fish

sellers bring the fish they have caught to market in buckets and

large bins. I like watching the surfers on the beach.

Sometimes the fish sellers will cook the fish for you. I like fish tacos

the best. The bus can take you to the city if you want to go there.

Fish tacos melt in your mouth.

Writing Project: Edit

Edit and Proofread

Use the Editing Marks to edit and proofread this paragraph. Look for:

- **compound subjects-verb agreement**
- **end marks**
- **compound words: regular and hyphenated.**

Editing Marks	
∧	Add.
℘	Delete.
⌒	Close up.

The fruit stall and fish stands is open at different times. The stalls selling clothes and other goods stays open until 8:00 P.M. The stalls with fruit, vegetables, and shell fish close by 4:00 P.M. If you want fresh food, it is best to get there early

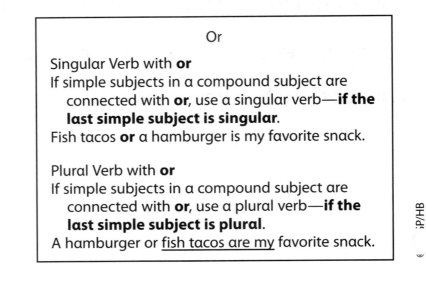

And

Plural Verb with **and**
If simple subjects in a compound subject are connected with **and**, use a plural verb.
Fish tacos and oranges **are** my favorite snack.

Or

Singular Verb with **or**
If simple subjects in a compound subject are connected with **or**, use a singular verb—**if the last simple subject is singular**.
Fish tacos **or** a hamburger is my favorite snack.

Plural Verb with **or**
If simple subjects in a compound subject are connected with **or**, use a plural verb—**if the last simple subject is plural**.
A hamburger or <u>fish tacos are my</u> favorite snack.

Name _____ Date _____

Catching the Light

Make a concept map with the answers to the Big Question:
What is the power of the sun?

What is
the power
of the sun?

Thinking Map: Character Chart

Our Characters

Character	Role	Function	Conflict

P/HB

Name _____   Date _____

The Fantastic Sun

Grammar Rules Different Kinds of Sentences

1. Use a statement to tell something.
2. Use a command to tell someone to do something.
3. Use an exclamation to show strong feeling. End it with an exclamation point.
4. Use a negative sentence to say "No" about something.
5. Use contractions to make two words into one word: can't won't, don't, doesn't, isn't, aren't.

Label each sentence to tell what type it is. Circle contractions.

1. The sun is fantastic! _____

2. I want to learn about the sun. _____

3. Get your coat. _____

4. I don't need a coat inside. _____

5. You can't learn about the sun here . _____

6. We will go to the library. _____

Tell your partner something about the sun. Use at least two kinds of sentences and one contraction.

SP & HB

Ten Suns

1

Long ago there were ten suns, the children of Di Jun and his wife Xi He. Each day, one of the suns walked across the sky, bringing warmth and light.

2

The suns were tired of following the same path across the sky. They decided to walk together. The heat of the ten suns began to burn the Earth.

3

Di Jun and Xi He called for their sons to come back, but they did not listen. Di Jun did not want the Earth destroyed, so he had the Archer of Heaven shoot down the suns. As each boy was hit by an arrow, he turned into a crow.

4

Di Jun realized that if all of the suns were destroyed, the Earth would be plunged into icy darkness. He left just one sun to heat the Earth.

P & HB
©

Grammar: Questions: *Yes/No* Answers; *Do/Does*

The Question Game

Grammar Rules Questions: *Yes/No* Answers; *Do/Does*

1. A question ends with a question mark.
2. A question can begin with the word *Do* or *Does*.
3. You may answer a question using *yes* or *no* and, if you wish, a contraction. For example: *No, I do not* or *No, I don't.*

Unscramble the words to ask a question. Then answer your question.

1. crows / Do / fly / ? _____

2. shine / the / sun / Does / ? _____

3. have / ten / Do / suns / we / ? _____

4. Does / a / sunlight / plant / absorb / ? _____
   _____

5. need / animals / Do / sunlight / ? _____
   _____

6. into / people / suns / turn / Do / ? _____
   _____

P/HB
©

Reread and Retell: Character Chart

Ten Suns

Character	Role	Function	Conflict
Di Jun	father		sons want to light the sky all at once
ten sons			

💬 **Use your chart to retell the myth to a partner.**

Fluency: Intonation

Use this passage to practice reading with proper intonation.

Ten Suns

Hu Yi refused. "How can I harm your boys? They are like my   13

children. I taught them to shoot with a bow and arrow. We both still   27

love them, even when they disobey."   33

"I love the creatures of Earth, too. I must protect them," Di Jun   46

told Hu Yi. "Do not be afraid. You will not harm the boys. My sons   61

will not be hurt, but they will be changed. Never again will they cross   75

the sky as suns. They will be gods no more. Hurry! Do as I command.   90

There is no time to spare. Earth is dying."   99

Intonation

B ☐ Does not change pitch.　　　　　A ☐ Changes pitch to match some of the content.

I ☐ Changes pitch, but does not match content.　　AH ☐ Changes pitch to match all of the content.

Accuracy and Rate Formula

Use the formula to measure a reader's accuracy and rate while reading aloud.

_____ − _____ = _____

words attempted　　　number of errors　　　words correct per minute
in one minute　　　　　　　　　　　　　　　(wcpm)

P/HB

©

Reading Options: Double-Entry Log

How the Fifth Sun Came to Be

Page	My Question	The Answer

P/HB

🗨 **How did you figure out the answers to your questions? Tell a partner.**

©

Respond and Extend: Comparison Chart

Compare Origin Myths

Comparison Chart

	"Ten Suns"	**"How the Fifth Sun Came to Be"**
Tell the type of myth.		Aztec
Tell what the myth explains.		
Setting		Mexico
List the characters.	**Gods** **Heroes:** **Other:**	**Gods** **Heroes:** **Other:**
Tell what the story is about.	**Beginning:** **Middle:** **End:**	**Beginning:** **Middle:** **End:**
Tell the story's message.		

P/HB

Ⓒ

Take turns with a partner. Share another message you think each myth has.

Grammar Rules: Kinds of Sentences

The Story of the Sun

Grammar Rules Kinds of Sentences

1. Use a statement to tell something.

2. Use a command to tell someone to do something.

3. Use an exclamation to show strong feeling. End it with an exclamation mark. (!)

4. Use a question to ask something. End it with a question mark. (?)

Follow the directions. Use a contraction in at least one sentence.

1. Write a statement about the sun's power.

   _____

2. Write an exclamation about the sun.

   _____

3. Write a question you have about the sun.

   _____

4. Write a command about staying safe in the sun.

   _____

Listen as a partner tells you something about the sun. Use a different kind of sentence to respond.

P/HB

©

Name _____ Date _____

A School Project

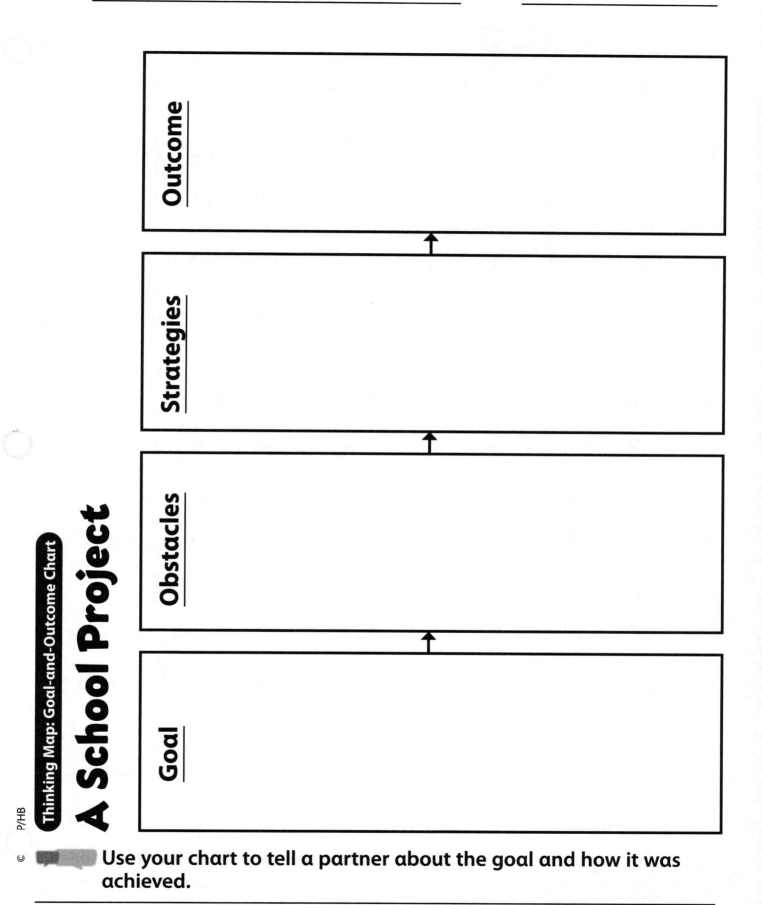

Goal	Obstacles	Strategies	Outcome

💬 **Use your chart to tell a partner about the goal and how it was achieved.**

Name _____ Date _____

Energy for Our Planet

Grammar Rules Compound Sentences

A compound sentence joins ideas with a comma plus a conjunction.

- Use **and** to join ideas that are alike.
- Use **but** to join ideas that are different.
- Use **or** to join ideas that show a choice.
- Use **so** to explain why.

Create a compound sentence from each pair of sentences.

1. Solar energy is powerful. Not enough people use its power.

   _____

2. Solar cells capture the sunlight. They use the light energy to

   create electricity. _____

   _____

3. Some electrical power plants get energy from coal. They can get

   it from oil. _____

   _____

P/HB

Tell a partner what you know about the sun. Have your partner tell you an idea, too. Combine your ideas into a compound sentence.

Name _____ Date _____

Thomas Culhane

1

Thomas Culhane teaches people about solar power. Very few people around the world use solar power, and he wants to change that.

2

Culhane went to Cairo, Egypt, to teach students how to use the sun's energy to make hot water. The students learned that there are many types of energy, including chemical energy, electrical energy, and light energy. Solar-powered water heaters use the sun's energy.

3

COLD WATER FLOWS TO THE BOTTOM OF THE PIPES

BLACK ALUMINUM FINS ABSORB HEAT AND TRANSFER IT TO THE PIPES

AS THE WATER WARMS, IT RISES THROUGH THE PIPES TO THE TOP OF THE TANK

The students built a water heater with large, black panels to absorb the sun's energy. That energy becomes the heat that warms the water pipes inside the panels. As the water inside the pipes gets warmer, it rises and moves through the pipes to a storage tank. A pipe carries the hot water down to the schoolyard.

Culhane told the students, "This is just the beginning!"

Grammar: Complex Sentences

Use Complex Sentences

Grammar Rule **Complex Sentences and Subordinate Conjunctions**

A complex sentence has one independent, or main, clause and at least one dependent clause.

Expand each independent clause by using the subordinating conjunction in parentheses to create a complex sentence. Say each sentence.

1. We can't understand the sun's importance _____

   _____ **(if)**

2. I am working when I move my body _____

   _____ **(because)**

3. I don't need to plug in my solar calculator _____

   _____ **(since)**

4. Chemical reactions occur inside my body _____ **(after)**

5. Atoms inside solar cells release electrons _____

   _____ **(when)**

P/HB

©

Name _____ Date _____

Energy for the Future

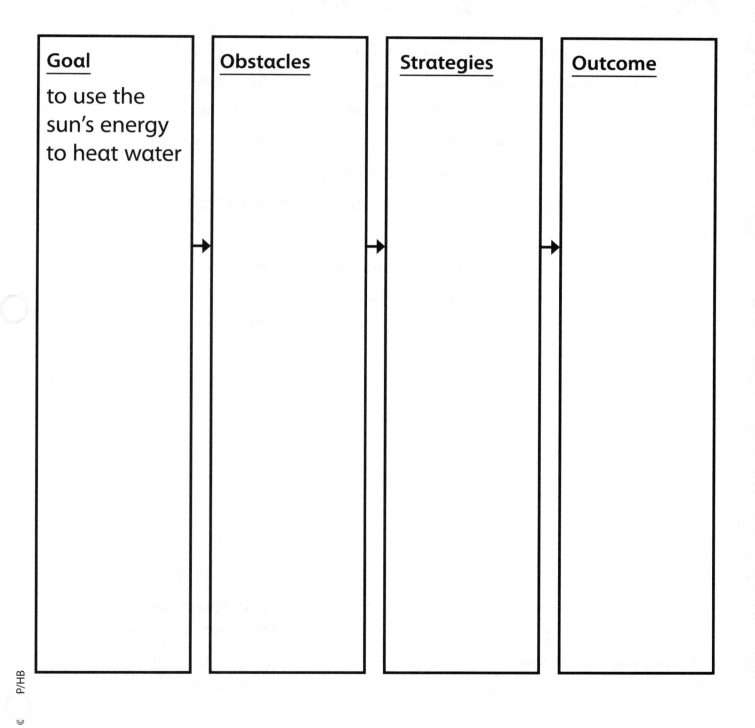

Goal	Obstacles	Strategies	Outcome
to use the sun's energy to heat water			

💬 **Use your chart to retell the selection to a partner.**

P/HB

©

Use this passage to practice reading with proper phrasing.

Energy For the Future

Today we had a problem. We tested our metal storage	10
tank. It leaked! Then one student had an idea. He took me to a place	25
where plastic barrels from a shampoo factory were being re-sold. The	36
barrels were inexpensive, and perfect for our hot water heaters.	46
When we returned, the students cheered. "But how will the water	57
in the tank stay hot?" asked one student. "Maybe it just needs a blanket,"	71
said another.	73
Clearly, the students have become energy problem-solvers. At	81
the end of the day today, we insulated our tank with a	93
"blanket" of fiberglass insulation, and then gave each other high-fives.	103

Phrasing

[B] ☐ Rarely pauses while reading the text.   [A] ☐ Frequently pauses at appropriate points in the text.

[I] ☐ Occasionally pauses while reading the text.   [AH] ☐ Consistently pauses at all appropriate points in the text.

Accuracy and Rate Formula

Use the formula to measure a reader's accuracy and rate while reading aloud.

$$\frac{\rule{3cm}{0.4pt}}{\substack{\text{words attempted} \\ \text{in one minute}}} - \frac{\rule{3cm}{0.4pt}}{\text{number of errors}} = \frac{\rule{3cm}{0.4pt}}{\substack{\text{words correct per minute} \\ \text{(wcpm)}}}$$

Name _____ Date _____

How to Make a Solar Oven

Page	My Question	The Answer

How did you figure out the answers to your questions?

© P/HB

Name _____   Date _____

Compare Online Documents

	"How to Make a Solar Oven"	"Energy for the Future"
Genre		
Point of View	first person ☐ second person ☐ third person ☐	first person ☐ second person ☐ third person ☐
Formal or Informal 1. Analyze the writing. 2. Check the boxes that tell about the writing. 3. Decide if the writing is formal or informal.	Did the writer use: slang ☐ exclamation points ☐ abbreviations ☐ questions ☐ conversational voice ☐ formal ☐ informal ☐	Did the writer use: slang ☐ exclamation points ☐ abbreviations ☐ questions ☐ conversational voice ☐ formal ☐ informal ☐

Talk with a partner about how the purpose of a blog is different from that of a how-to article.

Name _____   Date _____

Sun Baked Potatoes

Grammar Rules Compound and Complex Sentences

1. To make a compound sentence, use a comma and a conjunction (*and, but, or, so, yet,* or *nor*) to join two independent clauses.

2. Join a dependent clause with an independent clause to make a complex sentence. Use a comma if the dependent clause comes first. Use words such as *when, because, although, while,* and *since.*

Write compound and complex sentences.

_____ you can bake potatoes in an electric or gas oven, it's fun to bake them in the sun! A solar oven may be small _____ it does work. First, wash the potatoes _____ then put them in a pot. The pot must be black _____ it will not absorb enough heat from the sun to cook the potatoes. _____ your potatoes bake have fun. The pot won't burn _____ your potatoes will take about six hours to bake.

Write one compound and one complex sentence and share them with a partner.

Name _____   Date _____

Focus and Coherence

	Is the focus clear?	**Is the writing complete? Do the sentences fit together well?**
4 Wow!	• The plot is clear. • All the events and characters make sense for the plot.	• The writing feels complete. • The story has a clear beginning, middle, and end.
3 Ahh.	• The plot is fairly clear. • Most of the events and characters make sense for the plot.	• The writing feels mostly complete. • Parts of the beginning, middle, and end are clear.
2 Hmm.	• The plot is somewhat clear. • Some of the events and characters do not make sense for the plot.	• The writing feels somewhat complete. • The beginning, middle, and end are not all clear.
1 Huh?	• The plot is difficult to understand. • Few of the events and characters make sense for the plot.	• The writing feels incomplete. • The story has no beginning, middle, or end. It just has a few events.

Writing Project: Prewrite

Character Chart

Complete the Character Chart for your myth.

Character	Role	Function	Conflict

Revise

Use the Revising Marks to revise this paragraph. Look for:

- details that help develop the main idea
- varied sentence types.

Revising Marks	
∧	Add.
℘	Take out.
∧̬	Add a comma.
∧!	Add an exclamation mark.
∧?	Add a question mark.

Why Do We Have Tornados?

The world was young. Wolf and Rabbit were friends. Snake ate Rat. They did things together. they helped each other. Bananas are yellow.

They got into an argument one day. Crow flew away. Wolf said he was better. Rabbit said he was better. Wolf started to chase Rabbit.

Writing Project: Edit

Edit and Proofread

Use the Editing Marks to edit and proofread the paragraph. Look for:

- **different sentence types**
- **commas in compound and complex sentences**
- **correct spelling of contractions.**

Editing Marks	
∧	Add.
ℯ	Take out.
◯	Check spelling.
∧̫	Add a comma
∨̬	Add an apostrophe.
≡	Capitalize.

Why Do We Have Tornados? (continued)

Wolf chased Rabbit for days on end. finally Rabbit began to tire. and He realized that Wolf would eventually catch him. "I must think of a clever trick thought Rabbit."

Rabbit suddenly stopped. and as Wolf ran past Rabbit grabbed Wolf's tail as hard as he could. He wouldnt let go.

"Ive got him now!" laughed Wolf as he twisted around to nip at Rabbit. But no matter how far he twisted or how hard he tried Wolf couldnt quite reach Rabbit. they spun faster and faster until they stirred up a twisting wind. The wind blew so hard that it swept up rocks bushes and trees. Today we call this twisting wind a tornado. So when you hear about or see a tornado you know that Wolf is chasing Rabbit.

Name _____   Date _____

Nature's Network

Make a concept map with the answers to the Big Question:
What is nature's network?

What is
nature's
network?

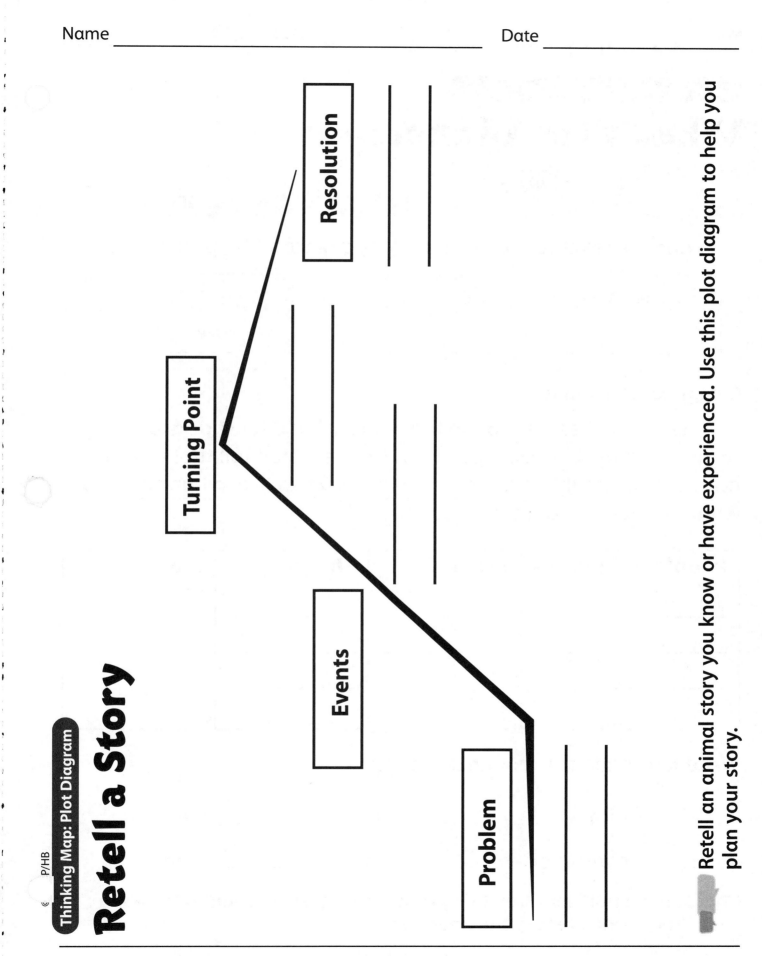

P/HB

Thinking Map: Plot Diagram

Retell a Story

Resolution

Turning Point

Events

Problem

Retell an animal story you know or have experienced. Use this plot diagram to help you plan your story.

Grammar: Nouns and Articles *a, an, the*

What's for Dinner?

Grammar Rules Nouns

A noun names a person or an animal, a place, a thing, or an idea.

Person or Animal	Place	Thing	Idea
owl	desert	sun	hunger

Categorize the nouns.

A <u>deer</u> searches for <u>food</u> in the <u>woods</u>. The deer snacks on tasty <u>twigs</u> and <u>blackberries</u>. A nearby <u>rabbit</u> feeds on tall <u>grass</u>. Since both deer and rabbits are <u>herbivores</u>, they can live in <u>harmony</u>. But what about other <u>animals</u> in the <u>forest</u>?

People or Animals	Places	Things	Idea
deer	_____	_____	_____
_____		_____	
_____		_____	
_____			

Write *a* or *an* in front of each noun.

_____ bird   _____ ant   _____ idea

_____ consumer   _____ egg   _____ plant

💬 **Tell a partner three things you have learned about nature's network. Identify the nouns you use.**

;P & HB

Key Points Reading

Coyote and Badger

There was a drought in Chaco Canyon. All the animals were hungry, even Coyote. He tried to hunt for prey, but he was too slow.

Badger and her pups were also hungry. Badger dug many holes to try to catch her prey, but she went home hungry, too.

One night Coyote heard Badger digging. A rat ran out of its hole. Coyote caught it. Another rat came up and saw Coyote. It went back down the hole. Badger caught it.

Outside the hole, Badger and Coyote sniffed and growled at each other. Then they relaxed. They formed a partnership. They began hunting together. It was much better than hunting alone.

The drought got worse. Coyote and Badger had to travel far to find food. One night, an eagle killed one of Badger's pups. Badger and her other pup went away.

Coyote had to hunt alone again. Then the rains came again. There would be more food for all the animals.

Grammar: Plural Nouns

The Make-It-Plural Game

Grammar Rules Plural Nouns

1. A noun names a person or an animal, a place, a thing, or an idea.
2. Add -*s* to form the plural of most nouns.
3. Add -*es* to form the plural of nouns that end in
   x, ch, sh, ss, z, and sometimes *o.*

1. **Play with a partner.**
2. **Spin the spinner.**
3. **Change the noun to a plural noun. Say a sentence that includes the plural noun.**

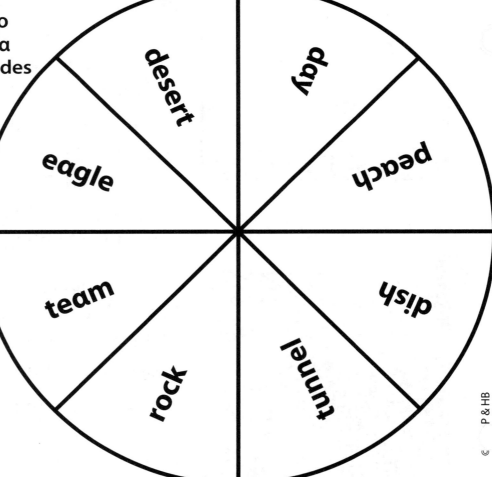

Make a Spinner

1. Push a paper clip ⊂⊃ through the center of the circle.

2. Hold one end of the paper clip with a pencil.

3. Spin the paper clip around the pencil.

© P & HB

Vocabulary: Apply Word Knowledge

Vocabulary Bingo

1. Write one Key Word under each plant.

2. Listen to the clues. Find the Key Word and use a marker to cover it.

3. Say "Bingo" when you have four markers in a row.

Reread and Retell: Plot Diagram

Coyote and Badger

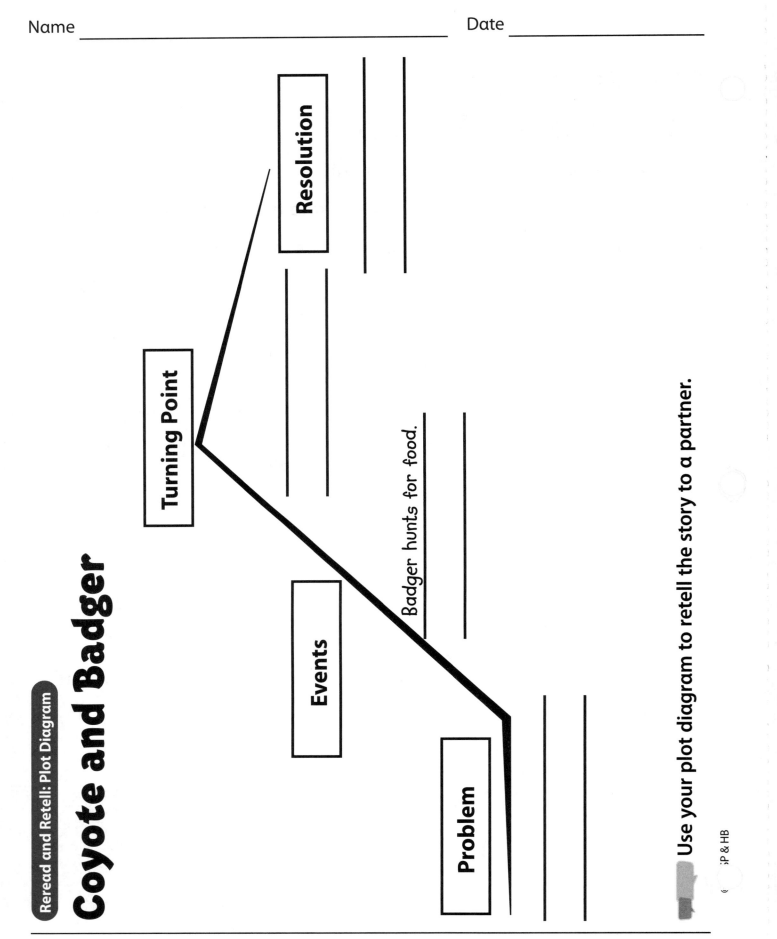

Turning Point

Resolution

Events

Badger hunts for food.

Problem

Use your plot diagram to retell the story to a partner.

;P & HB

Fluency: Intonation

Use this passage to practice reading with proper intonation.

Coyote and Badger

  Farther up the canyon, Badger emerged from her den. She left her two   13
pups safely underground and waddled off as the air began to cool.   25
Badger was a night hunter, too, but she seldom chased rabbits.   36
She was a digger, not a runner.   43

  When Badger found the hole of an antelope squirrel, she tore into the   56
hard soil with her long claws. The dirt flew, and in a wink she was   71
underground following a dark tunnel. No animal can dig as fast as   83
a badger, but the squirrel raced ahead and escaped.   92

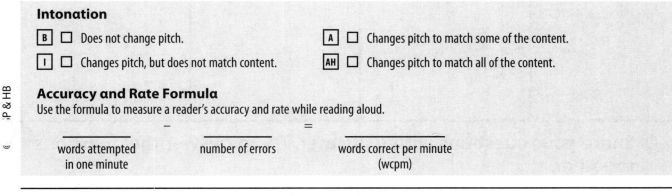

Intonation

B ☐ Does not change pitch.   A ☐ Changes pitch to match some of the content.

I ☐ Changes pitch, but does not match content.   AH ☐ Changes pitch to match all of the content.

Accuracy and Rate Formula
Use the formula to measure a reader's accuracy and rate while reading aloud.

$$\underline{\hspace{3cm}} - \underline{\hspace{3cm}} = \underline{\hspace{3cm}}$$

 words attempted   number of errors   words correct per minute
  in one minute   (wcpm)

P & HB

Name _____ Date _____

Living Links

K What I Know	W What I Want To Learn	L What I Learned	Q Questions I Still Have

💬 **Share your questions with a partner. Try to answer the questions together.**

SP & HB

Respond and Extend: Food Web

Compare Content

Add the names of plants and animals from "Coyote and Badger" to correct places in the food web.

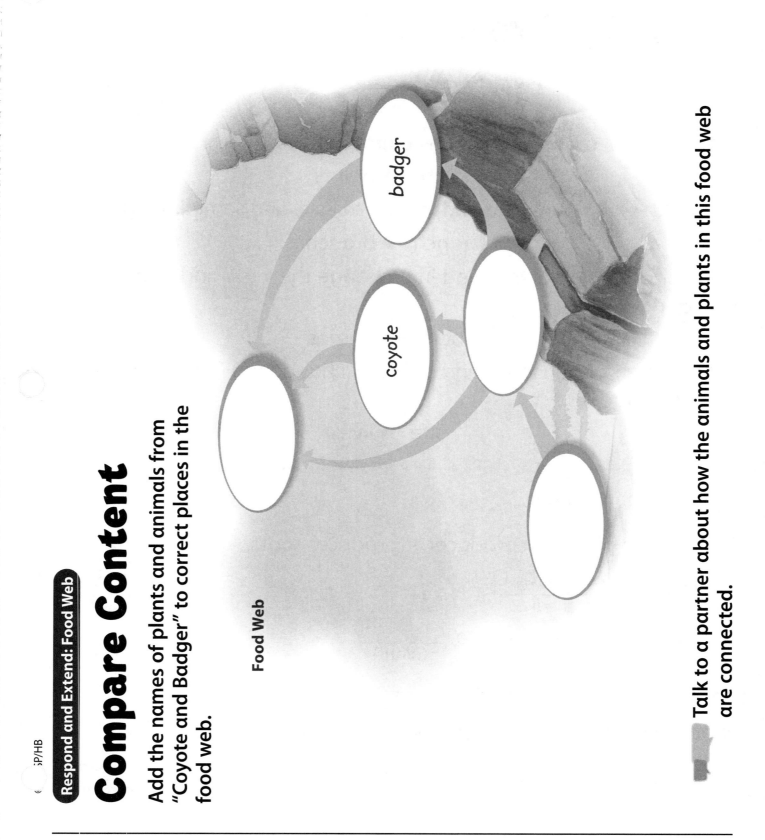

Food Web

coyote

badger

▬ Talk to a partner about how the animals and plants in this food web are connected.

Grammar: Plural Nouns

What Do They Eat?

Grammar Rules Plural Nouns

1. Add -s to make most nouns plural.

plant → plant**s**

2. Add -es to nouns that end in *x, ch, sh, ss, z,* and sometimes *o.*

branch → branch**es**

3. For **most** nouns that end in *y,* change the *y* to *i* and then add -es.

berry → berr**ies**

4. For **most** nouns that end in *f* or *fe,* change the *f* or *fe* to *v* and then add -es.

life → li**ves**

Write the plural nouns.

1. A potato plant is a producer. It produces roots,

stems, and ___*leaves*___ .
　　　　　(leaf)

2. Some animals eat potato _____ .
　　　　　　　　　　　　　(plant)

3. They need the energy in the _____ to survive.
　　　　　　　　　　　　　　　(potato)

4. Animals like _____ also eat other animals.
　　　　　　　　(fox)

5. Eagles sometimes eat badger _____ .
　　　　　　　　　　　　　　(baby)

P & HB

Thinking Map: Tree Diagram

Small Things, Big Idea!

Write a main idea about your small plant or animal on the left side of the tree diagram. List details that support that idea on the right.

Main Idea   **Details**

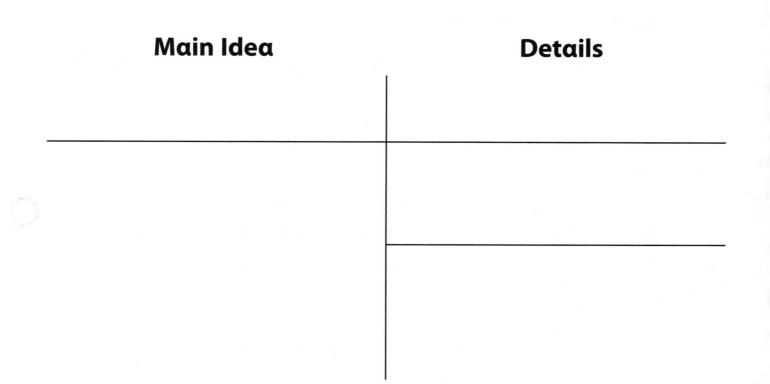

Use your tree diagram to track the main idea and details your partner gives about why a small plant or animal is important.

Name _____ Date _____

Living Things

Grammar Rules Count/Noncount Nouns

Nouns that you can count have a singular form and a plural form. Nouns that you cannot count have the same form for "one" and "more than one."

Count Nouns	Noncount Nouns
birds, flowers	prey, weather

Categorize the nouns.

Scientists who study biology learn about living things like plants and animals. All living things need energy. Plants use sunlight, water, and nutrients to get energy. This is known as photosynthesis. Many animals eat plants to get energy.

Count Nouns	Noncount Nouns
Scientists	_____
_____	_____
_____	_____
_____	_____
_____	_____

Use three of the nouns above. Tell a partner something about nature.

5P & HB

Name _____ Date _____

Fish of the Future

1

Dr. Tierney Thys studies the ocean's ecosystem. She focuses on the sunfish. She believes understanding how the ocean environment is connected is crucial for its survival.

2

Sunfish Size Comparisons		
Animal	Average Length	Average Weight
sea lion	2.7 m (9 ft)	566 kg (1,248 lbs)
sunfish	1.8 m (6 ft)	999 kg (2,202 lbs)
great white shark	4.6 m (15 ft)	2,268 kg (5,000 lbs)
blue whale	29.9 m (98 ft)	99,800 kg (220,021 lbs)

The sunfish holds three world records. As it grows, it increases in weight more than other vertebrates. It is the world's heaviest bony fish. It produces more eggs at one time than any other vertebrate.

3

Overfishing is reducing the numbers of fish. Jellyfish compete with other fish for food. Because it eats jellyfish, the sunfish may keep their population under control.

4

Dr. Thys says the sunfish may be the fish of the future. It shows us that all creatures have a place in the world and that it's important to keep the ocean system whole.

P & HB

Name _____   Date _____

The Irregulars

Grammar Rules Irregular Plurals

Some words have special spellings for "more than one."

foot ⟶ feet

Match each noun with its irregular plural.

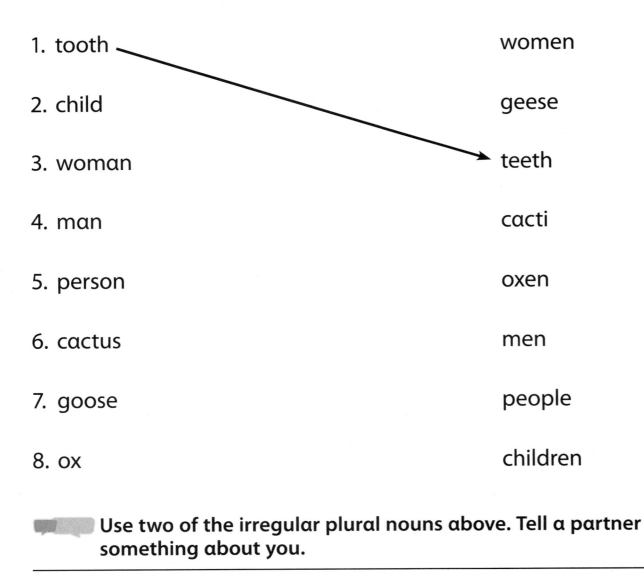

1. tooth   women

2. child   geese

3. woman   teeth

4. man   cacti

5. person   oxen

6. cactus   men

7. goose   people

8. ox   children

▬▬▬ **Use two of the irregular plural nouns above. Tell a partner something about you.**

Reread and Summarize: Tree Diagram

Fish of the Future

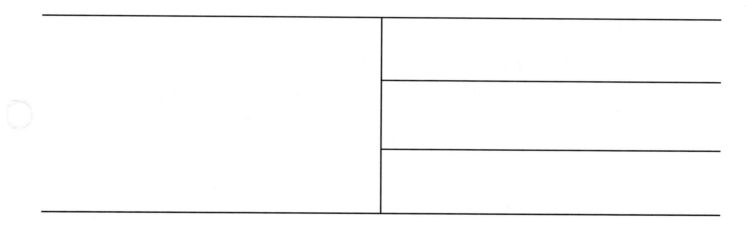

p. 194–196 What's special about the sunfish?	It has a strange body shape.
	It lies on its side at the ocean's surface as if it's sunning itself.
	It has a beak-like mouth.
	It is covered with parasites.

💬 Use your tree diagram to summarize the interview to a partner.

SP & HB

Name _____ Date _____

Use this passage to practice reading with proper expression.

Fish of the Future

The sunfish holds three world records! As it grows, the sunfish increases	12
in weight more than any other vertebrate—up to 60 million times its	25
size at hatching. If you grew that much, you'd be as big as 30 thousand	40
school buses!	42
Second, it is the world's heaviest bony fish. The heaviest sunfish ever recorded	55
weighed more than 2,300 kilograms (over 5,000 pounds). That's as heavy as	67
ten grand pianos, or five large cows!	74
Third, the sunfish produces more eggs at one time than any other vertebrate.	87
Scientists found one mother sunfish carrying an estimated 300 million eggs.	99

Expression

B ☐ Does not read with feeling.　　　　A ☐ Reads with appropriate feeling for most content.

I ☐ Reads with some feeling, but does not match content.　AH ☐ Reads with appropriate feeling for all content.

Accuracy and Rate Formula

Use the formula to measure a reader's accuracy and rate while reading aloud.

_____ − _____ = _____

words attempted　　　number of errors　　　words correct per minute
in one minute　　　　　　　　　　　　　　　　(wcpm)

P/HB

Phyto-Power!

That's Amazing!

An amazing fact about _____

is _____

_____

I found it in the book _____

by _____

_____   _____

Name   Date

That's Amazing!

An amazing fact about _____

is _____

_____

I found it in the book _____

by _____

_____   _____

Name   Date

Tell a partner which fact was your favorite and why.

Name _____   Date _____

Compare Genres

Use this chart to compare "Phyto-Power" with "Fish of the Future."

	Science Article	Interview
Purpose Is the purpose to inform, entertain, or persuade?		
Text Structure	**Main Idea and Details**	**Question and Answer**
	Photos	Photos
	Tables	Tables
	Charts	Charts
	Illustrations	Illustrations
	Headings	Headings
	Maps	Maps
	Diagrams	Diagrams

Take turns with a partner. Ask each other questions about an interview or a science article.

Grammar: More Plural Nouns

The Make-It-Plural Game

Grammar Rules Plurals Nouns

1. Some nouns are the same for "one" and "more than one."

   a grain of sand → all the grains of sand

2. Some nouns have special spellings for "more than one."

   one mouse → two mice

3. Collective nouns name groups of people or things. To make these nouns plural, add -s or -es.

   one collection of seashells → two collections of seashells

1. **Play with a partner.**
2. **Spin the spinner.**
3. **Change the noun to a plural noun. If the plural form is the same as the singular, say: *same form*. Say a sentence using the plural noun.**

Make a Spinner

1. Put a paper clip ▭ through the center of the circle.
2. Hold one end of the paper clip with a pencil.
3. Spin the paper clip around the pencil.

SP & HB

class
crew
chlorophyll
woman
club
health
litter
leaf

Name _____   Date _____

Organization

	Is the whole thing organized?	Does the writing flow?
4 Wow!	The writing is very well organized. It fits the writer's purpose.	The order of questions and answers makes sense. The questions flow well.
3 Ahh.	The writing is organized. It fits the writer's purpose.	The writing is pretty smooth. There are only a few places where it jumps around.
2 Hmm.	The writing is organized, but it doesn't fit the writer's purpose.	The writing jumps from one question to another idea, but I can follow it a little.
1 Huh?	The writing is not organized. Maybe the writer forgot to use a chart to plan.	I can't tell what the writer wants to say.

Name _____   Date _____

Chart

Complete the chart for your interview.

	Questions	**Answers**
Who?		
What?		
Where?		
When?		
Why?		
How?		

P/HB

Writing Project: Revise

Revise

Use the Revising Marks to revise this paragraph. Look for:

- **a detailed introduction**
- **a logical organization**

Revising Marks

∧	Add.
℘	Take out.
⊂⌐	Move to here.
⊂⊃	Check spelling.
≡	Capitalize.

Liz Fox

She has anno delete mark through it. She is a Wildlife Rescue volunteer. I asked her about opossums.

Q. Are opossums dangerous?

A. Opossums are shy creatures. However, they can carry rabies even when they do not look sick. So, if a person sees an opossum, it is best to leave it alone.

Q. What kind of animals are opossums?

A. Opossums are marsupials. they carry their young in pouches like kangaroos.

Q. What do opossums eat?

A. Opossums have a varied diet. They love to eat cat or dog food if it is available!

Writing Project: Edit

Edit and Proofread

Use the Editing Marks to edit and proofread these interview questions and answers. Look for:

- **correct spelling of plural nouns**
- **correct spelling of irregular plural nouns**
- **correct capitalization and punctuation of proper and possessive nouns.**

Editing Marks

∧	Add.
℘	Take out.
⬭⟋	Move to here.
⬭	Check spelling.
≡	Capitalize.
⟩∧	Add an apostrophe.

Q. What does an opossum's look like?

A. Adult opossums are nearly two foot long (about 20 inchs) and can weigh up to ten pounds. An opossums long, hairless tail helps it hang from tree's. When frightened, it will often hiss and show its 50 sharp tooth.

Q. Ms. fox, what should a person do if he or she finds an injured opossum?

A. You could contact your local wildlife rescue organization. Volunteer's can often help injured opossum's and return them to the wild.

SP/HB

Justice

**Make a concept map with the answers to the Big Question:
What is justice?**

Thinking Map: Theme

TV Show: _____

Theme Chart

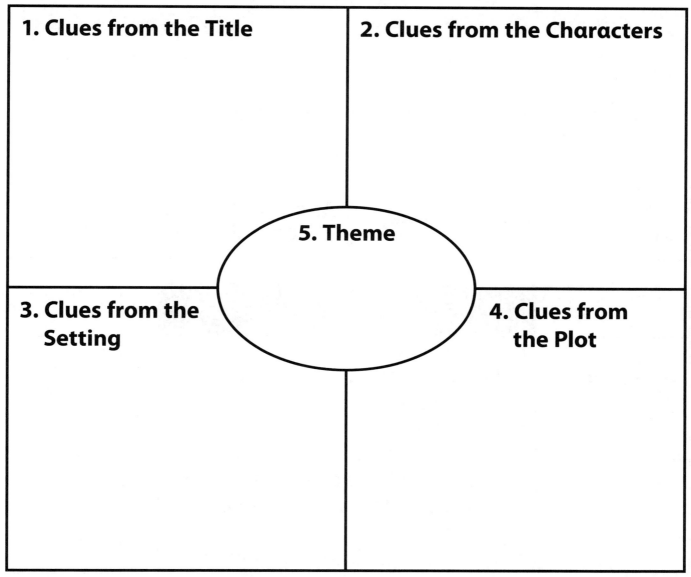

1. Clues from the Title	2. Clues from the Characters
3. Clues from the Setting	5. Theme	4. Clues from the Plot

Talk with a partner about a television show you have seen about a hero. Together, decide what you think the theme is.

SP/HB

Grammar: Present-Tense Action Verbs

The Action Game

Grammar Rules Present-Tense Action Verbs

Present-tense action verbs tell what people or things do *now*.

A woman <u>speaks</u>.   Manny and Maya <u>cheer</u>.   The bell <u>rings</u>.

Maria and Mark	We	miss	Ana and Lee	The woman	write
try					lifts
Salvator					The speaker
announce					waits
Diego					She
talk					They
BEGIN		**THE END**	climb	He	reads

How to Play the Action Game

1. Play with a partner.
2. Flip a coin. Move 1 space for heads. Move 2 spaces for tails.
3. Read the word. If it is a subject, use it in a sentence with a present-tense verb. If it is a verb, use it in a sentence with a subject that agrees with it.
4. Write you sentences on another sheet of paper.
5. The first one to reach THE END wins.

Crossing Bok Chitto

1

Bok Chitto was a river that separated the Choctaw from the plantations. One day, Martha Tom was looking for blackberries. She couldn't find any on her side, so she crossed the river. She walked on a secret stone path that lay just below the surface. Soon she was lost. A boy named Little Mo helped her home.

2

Little Mo's mother was to be sold. He wanted his family to cross Bok Chitto and escape. Little Mo asked Martha Tom for help. The Choctaw women dressed in white and held candles. The guards pointed their guns, but they never fired. They thought they saw a girl walking on water.

3

Martha Tom led Little Mo's family across the river. Their descendants still remember that night. The Choctaw speak of a girl's bravery. The dark-skinned people speak of a boy's faith. The white people speak of how seven enslaved people walked on water to freedom.

P & HB

© NGSP/HB

Grammar: Action Verbs: Present Progressive

Freedom

Grammar Rules **Action Verbs: Present Progressive**

1. A present-tense verb tells about action happening now.

2. Present-progressive verb phrases tell about action in progress.

3. Form the present progressive by adding the present-tense form of the verb *be* to the present participle.

Example: *We are walking.*

Replace each underlined verb with a present-progressive verb phrase.

The enslaved people <u>work</u> _____ hard on the plantation.

They <u>dream</u> _____ of finding freedom. A Choctaw child <u>plays</u>

_____ nearby. She <u>decides</u> _____ to help the enslaved

people. As they walk in the forest, she <u>tells</u> _____ them about a

plan.

The following week, someone on the plantation <u>helps</u> _____

the workers. The guards do not see what <u>happens</u> _____,

so the people <u>race</u> _____ away on a secret path. The plan is so

good that the people escape to freedom.

Name _____ Date _____

Crossing Bok Chitto

Theme Chart

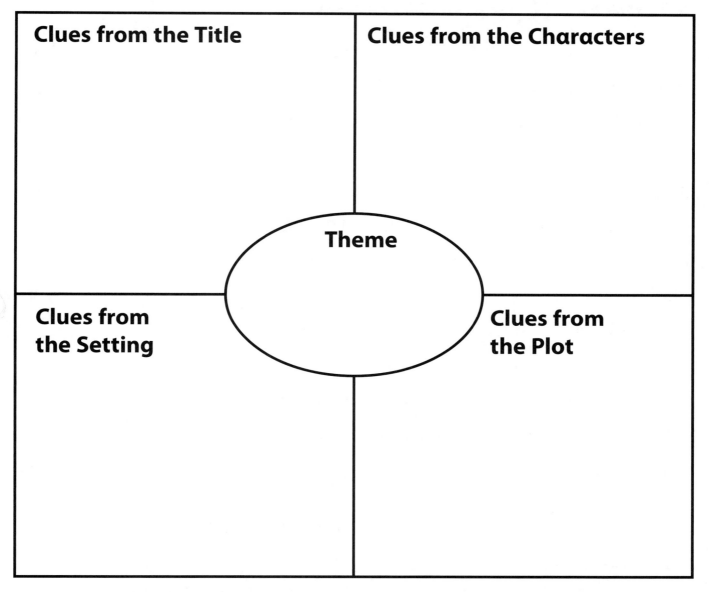

Clues from the Title

Clues from the Characters

Theme

Clues from the Setting

Clues from the Plot

💬 **Use your theme chart to retell the story to a partner.**

SP/HB

Fluency: Expression

Use this passage to practice reading with proper expression.

Crossing Bok Chitto

Then one day trouble came. Twenty enslaved people	8
were going to be sold. The men were called together to	19
listen to the names being read. Little Mo's mother was on	30
that list.	32
Little Mo's father wondered how to tell his family.	41
After supper, he motioned for them to be still. Feeling	51
his knees grow weak, he said, "Your mother has been	61
sold."	62
"Nooo!" she cried. The children began to cry, too.	71
"This is our last evening together!" he said. "Stop your	81
crying. I want every one of you to find something small	92
and precious to give your mother to remember you by."	102
No one moved.	105

From "Crossing Bok Chitto," page 239

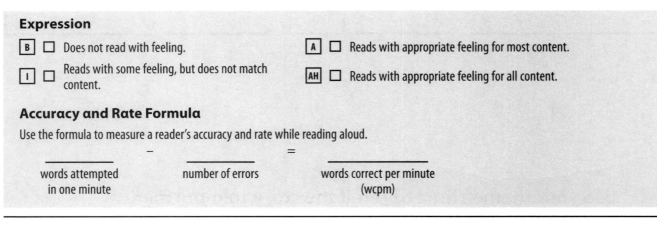

Expression

B ☐ Does not read with feeling.   A ☐ Reads with appropriate feeling for most content.

I ☐ Reads with some feeling, but does not match content.   AH ☐ Reads with appropriate feeling for all content.

Accuracy and Rate Formula

Use the formula to measure a reader's accuracy and rate while reading aloud.

_____ − _____ = _____

words attempted   number of errors   words correct per minute
in one minute   (wcpm)

Reading Options: Fact Cards

Journey to Freedom.

List three interesting facts you read about in "Journey to Freedom."

That's a fact!

One interesting fact I read about is _____ .

Another interesting fact I read about is _____ .

One more interesting fact I read about is _____ .

💬 **Tell a partner which fact was most interesting and why.**

SP\HB

Name _____ Date _____

Compare Figurative Language

"Crossing Bok Chitto"	"Journey to Freedom"
Quick as a bird, Little Mo flew across the stones. In my mind, I can see Little Mo hopping quickly across the stones.	Enslaved people who were running away often traveled hundreds of miles to reach freedom. In my mind, I can see the people arriving at a safe place.
Little Mo thought the music must be **the heartbeat of the earth itself.** In my mind, I can feel _____ _____	
Martha Tom knew her mother **could cackle like a crow** when she was angry. In my mind, I can hear _____ _____	As the runaways moved from **one station to the next, they were accompanied by a "conductor"** who made sure they arrived safely at the next destination. In my mind, I can see _____ _____ _____

🗨 Take turns with a partner. Share figurative language you liked in each selection. Tell your partner which selection was easier to "see" in your mind.

P/HB
©

Grammar Rules: Present-Tense Action Verbs

Stories on the Wall

Grammar Rules Present-Tense Action Verbs

1. Use a **present-tense verb** if the action is happening now, or if it happens all the time.

2. Some action verbs show action that you can't see.

3. In a sentence, the verb must agree with the subject of the sentence.

   Add -s to the verb when the subject is one person or thing.

   Do not add -s when the subject is more than one person or thing.

Write the correct form of the verb in parentheses.

1. These people _____ (care, cares) about justice.

2. The town museum _____ (show, shows) this.

3. One whole room _____ (tell, tells) stories about justice.

4. We _____ (visit, visits) the museum every year.

5. My little brother _____ (read, reads) the stories on the wall.

Listen when a partner tells you a subject. Choose the right present-tense action verb form for that subject. Together, make a sentence with the subject and verb.

PHB ©

Name _____ Date _____

Problems? Negotiate!

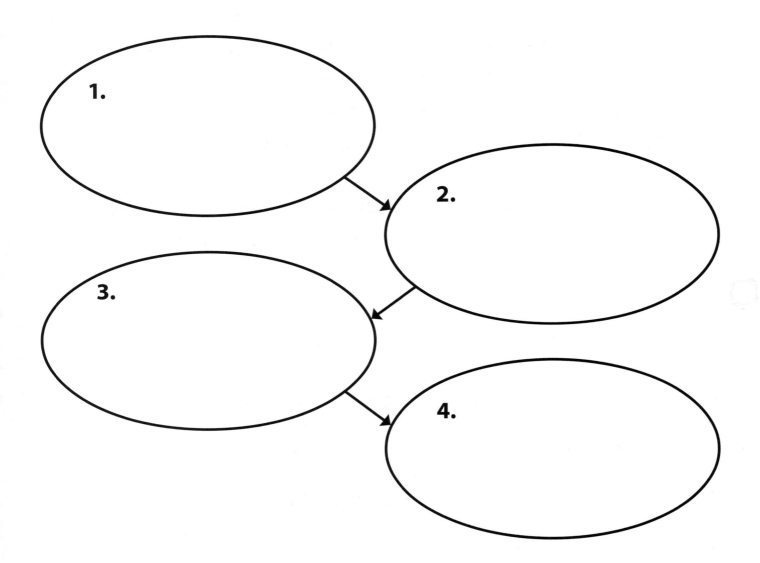

1.

2.

3.

4.

💬 **Tell your partner about something you negotiated. Your partner writes the sequence of the negotiation in the sequence chain above.**

Grammar: Verbs *am, is, are*

The Strike

Grammar Rules Verbs *am, is, are*

1. Use *am, is, are* to:
   - link the subject to a word in the predicate.
   - tell about an action that is happening.
   - come after the words *here* or *there*.
   - make the contractions *I'm, you're, he's, she's it's, we're, they're.*
2. The verb always agrees with the subject of the sentence.

Write *am, is, are, I'm, you're, he's, we're,* or *they're* in the blank.

Today ___ the day the workers ___ going on strike. I have never seen a strike, but ___ sure there are many good reasons for the strike. I ___ looking at the workers.

All of the workers ___ ready. One worker ___ speaking at a microphone. ____ telling the strikers to march for their rights.

They ___ marching in front of the store. There ___ many workers. _____ carrying signs.

There ___ one worker marching near me. I ask him why they ___ on strike.

"We ___ asking for higher pay. _____ working under poor conditions," he says and then marches on.

Role-play the last four lines of the story with a partner. One partner asks why the workers are on strike. The other tells why. Switch roles and repeat.

Name _____   Date _____

Harvesting Hope

1

César Chávez lived on a ranch in Arizona. When he was ten, his family lost the ranch. They went to California to look for work and became migrant workers. It was hard, painful work.

2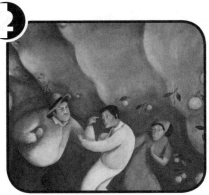

The landowners treated the workers poorly. There was no clean water. There were no rest breaks or bathrooms. Anyone who complained was fired, beaten up, or murdered. In his early 20s, César began to fight for change.

3

César organized meetings. He was shy, but he could solve problems. He encouraged truth instead of violence. Soon the National Farm Workers Association was formed.

4

To protest low pay, César organized a march. When the march reached Sacramento, 10,000 people had joined it. The vineyard owner signed a better contract. It was victory, but there was still much work ahead.

Grammar: Verbs *have* and *has*

Complete It

Grammar Rules *have* and *has*

1. Use **has** when you tell about one other person or thing. **Has** becomes **'s** when you form a contraction.
2. Use **have** with all other subjects. **Have** becomes **'ve** when you form a contraction.
3. Use **has** and **have** as a helping verb with an **-ed** verb.

1. **Play with a partner.**
2. **Spin the spinner.**
3. **Complete the sentence.**
4. **Take one point for completing a sentence correctly.**

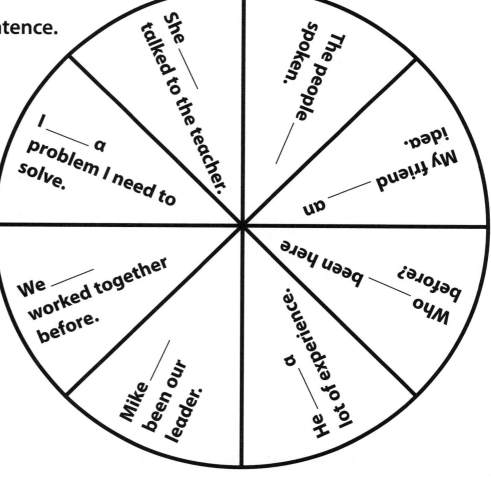

Make a Spinner
1. Put a paper clip  in the center of the circle.
2. Hold one end of the paper clip with a pencil.
3. Spin the paper clip around the pencil.

Reread and Retell: Sequence Chain

Harvesting Hope: The Story of César Chávez

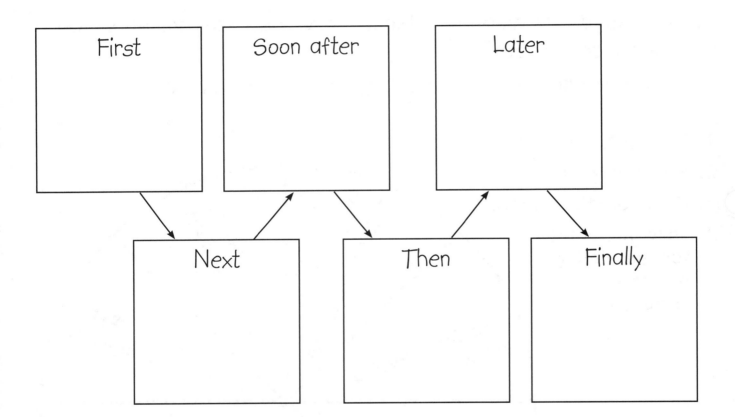

First

Soon after

Later

Next

Then

Finally

💬 **Use your sequence chain to retell the selection to a partner.**

P/HB

Fluency: Phrasing

Use this passage to practice reading with proper phrasing.

Harvesting Hope: The Story of César Chávez

Until César Chávez was ten, every summer night was like a *fiesta*.   12
César and his brothers, sisters, and cousins settled down to sleep   24
outside, under netting to keep mosquitoes out. But who could sleep,   35
with uncles and aunts singing and telling tales of life back in Mexico?   48

César Chávez thought the whole world belonged to his family.   58
The eighty acres of their ranch were an island in the shimmering   70
Arizona desert, and the starry skies were all their own.   80

César's grandfather had built their large adobe house to last forever.   91
A vegetable garden, cows, and chickens supplied all the food they   102
could want. With hundreds of cousins on farms nearby, there was   113
always someone to play with.   118

From "Harvesting Hope: The Story of César Chávez," page 264

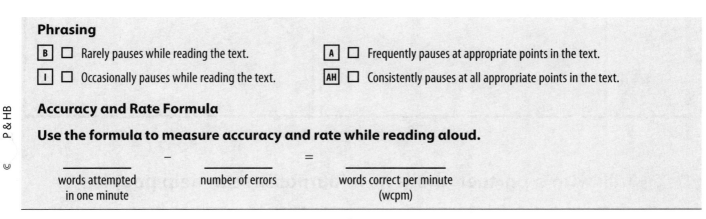

Phrasing

B ☐ Rarely pauses while reading the text.   A ☐ Frequently pauses at appropriate points in the text.

I ☐ Occasionally pauses while reading the text.   AH ☐ Consistently pauses at all appropriate points in the text.

Accuracy and Rate Formula

Use the formula to measure accuracy and rate while reading aloud.

_____ − _____ = _____
words attempted   number of errors   words correct per minute
in one minute   (wcpm)

P & HB
©

Reading Options: Reflection Journal

A Filmmaker for Justice

Page	My Question	The Answer

P & HB

💬 **Talk with a partner about how journalism can help people.**

Respond and Extend: Comparison Chart

Compare Literary Language

	"A Filmmaker for Justice"	"Harvesting Hope"
Similes	p. 281	p. 264 Every summer night was like
Metaphors	p. 284	The eighty acres of their ranch were an island in the shimmering Arizona desert.
Imagery	p. 284 work for change	pp. 264–265 singing, happy,
Foreshadowing	p. 282	p. 268 or p. 269

Take turns with a partner. Make up a simile and a metaphor.

P/HB

Name _____ Date _____

Bus Strike

Grammar Rules Forms of *be* and *have*

1. For yourself, use *am* or *have.*
2. When you tell about another person or a thing, use *is* or *has.*
3. For yourself <u>and</u> one or more people, use *are* or *have.*
4. When you tell about other people and things, use *are* or *have.*
5. For linking verbs, use *am, is,* and *are* to link the subject to a word in the predicate.
6. For helping verbs, use *am, is,* and *are* with *-ing* verbs, and *has* or *have* with *-ed* verbs.

Write the correct forms of *be* and *have*. If a subject is also needed in the sentence, use a contraction.

A news reporter ____ just arrived at the bus headquarters. Drivers ____ unhappy and they ____ decided to strike. The reporter interviewed the spokesperson for the drivers. She asked, "Why ____ you protesting?"

The spokesperson replied, "We ____ all doing the same job, but some drivers earn more than others. We ____ asked for equal pay, but the officials ____ not agreed. So, ____ decided to strike until our demand for equal pay ____ met.

> Pick a form of *be* and a form of *have* and write two new sentences. Use a contraction in one of the sentences. Read your sentences to a partner.

Writing Project: Rubric

Organization

	Is the whole thing organized?	How smoothly do the ideas flow together?
4 Wow!	• The writing is very well-organized. It fits the writer's purpose.	• The writing is very smooth. Each idea flows into the next one.
3 Ahh.	• The writing is organized. It fits the writer's purpose.	• The writing is pretty smooth. There are only a few places where it jumps around.
2 Hmm.	• The writing is organized, but it doesn't fit the writer's purpose.	• The writing jumps from one idea to the other, but I can follow it a little.
1 Huh?	• The writing is not organized. Maybe the writer forgot to make a plan.	• I can't tell what the writer wants to say.

P/HB

Name _____ Date _____

Brainstorm Your Topic

Use this chart to brainstorm possible topics for your research report. After you complete it, circle the topic that is most interesting to you.

Event	When It Happened	Who Was Involved

© P & HB

Writing Project: Source Cards

Source Cards

Create a source card for each source.

Title:	card number:
Author:	
Publication information:	
Library call number or Web address:	

Title:	card number:
Author:	
Publication information:	
Library call number or Web address:	

SP/HB

Writing Project: Outline

Outline

Use your note cards to create an outline. Use Arabic numbers (1, 2, 3) to add more details under your supporting points.

I.

   A.

   B.

   C.

II.

   A.

   B.

   C.

III.

   A.

   B.

   C.

IV.

   A.

   B.

   C.

SP & HB

Revise

Use the Revising Marks to revise these paragraphs. Look for:

- an order that makes sense
- the writer's own words.

Revising Marks

∧	Add.
ℐ	Take out.
⌒⟋	Move to here.

Dr. Héctor P. García

Dr. Héctor Pérez García fought for his rights. Dr. García was a doctor. He was also a hero in World War II. He founded a group called American GI Forum. He believed that everyone should have the same rights.

There was a time when Dr. García's wife and daughter were not welcomed in a café. In south Texas, Mexican Americans were treated unfairly. Dr. García said, "We had segregated schools, segregated campuses, segregated hospitals."

Dr. García's name would be forever interspersed with the names of heroes in the annals of history.

P/HB
©

Writing Project: Edit

Edit and Proofread

Use the Editing Marks to edit and proofread the paragraph and source list. Look for:

- subject-verb agreement
- words with suffixes spelled correctly
- correct punctuation and capitalization in a source list.

Editing Marks

∧	Add.
℘	Take out.
◯⌒∧	Move to here.

After Felix Longoria was killed in World War II, the funeral director in his hometown did not allow his body to be in the funeral home. Longoria's wife talked to Dr. Garcia. With his help, Felix Longoria became the first Mexican American to receive a hero's buryal in Arlington National Cemetery.

Dr. Garcia's organization continue   to help many Mexican Americans get justice. Garcia are a true hero.

Sources

Allsup, V. Carl. Felix longoria Affair. *The New handbook of Texas.* 1996. Print.

Felts, Jeff. "justice for My people: The dr. Héctor p García Story Corpus Christi: KEDT-Public Television. 2009. <http://www.justiceformypeople.org/index.html>

Garcia, Ignacio M. Héctor P. garcía: *In Relentless Pursuit of Justice.* houston: Arte Público Press, 2002.

P & HB
©

Name _____ Date _____

Every Drop

**Make a concept map with the answers to the Big Question:
Why is water so important?**

Why is water so important?

P & HB
©

Thinking Map: Main Idea and Details

The Drought

I. _____

    A. _____

    B. _____

II. _____

    A. _____

    B. _____

III. _____

    A. _____

    B. _____

Talk with a partner about ways water is important to Elena's family.

Grammar: Adjectives

Water Worries

Grammar Rules Adjectives

1. Add *-er* to an adjective to compare two things.
2. Add *-est* to an adjective to compare three or more things.

Complete each sentence. Add *-er* or *-est* to the word below the line.

1. Our farm is the _____ one in our area.
   <u>old</u>

2. Our well is by far the _____.
   <u>deep</u>

3. This year the water level was _____ than it should be.
   <u>low</u>

4. We were worried our crops would be _____ than they were
   <u>small</u>
   last year.

5. Luckily, our corn grew _____ than we thought it would.
   <u>tall</u>

With a partner, change each sentence with an *-er* word to a sentence with an *-est* word.

SP/HB

One Well

1

Most of the Earth's surface is covered with water. Surface water is found in oceans, lakes, rivers, and streams.

There is also groundwater. It fills the spaces between rocks, sand, and soil.

2

Water goes through the water cycle. It evaporates into the air. As the water vapor rises, it forms tiny droplets and then becomes clouds. When the droplets get too heavy, they fall as rain or snow.

3

Plants depend on water for transpiration and photosynthesis. Animals depend on water to aid digestion, remove waste, and control temperature.

4

Not all water is accessible. Most of the water on Earth is saltwater. The distribution of fresh water across the world is not equal. Many people do not have enough fresh water. Taking action to conserve the water supply will help protect it for everyone.

SP/HB

Grammar: Comparative Adjectives

The Adjective Game

Grammar Rules Adjectives

1. To compare two things, use *more . . . than* or *less . . . than* if an adjective has three or more syllables.

2. When you compare three or more things, use *most* or *least* if the adjective has three or more syllables.

3. Some adjectives have special forms for comparing things. For example: *good, better, best.*

1. **Play with a partner.**

2. **Spin the spinner.**

3. **Read the adjective. Use it to compare either two things or three or more things.**

Make a Spinner

1. Put a paper clip ⊂⊃ in the center of the circle.

2. Hold one end of the paper clip with a pencil.

3. Spin the paper clip around the pencil.

Vocabulary Bingo

1. **Write one Key Word in each square.**

2. **Listen to the clues. Find the Key Word and use a marker to cover it.**

3. **Say "Bingo" when you have four markers in a row.**

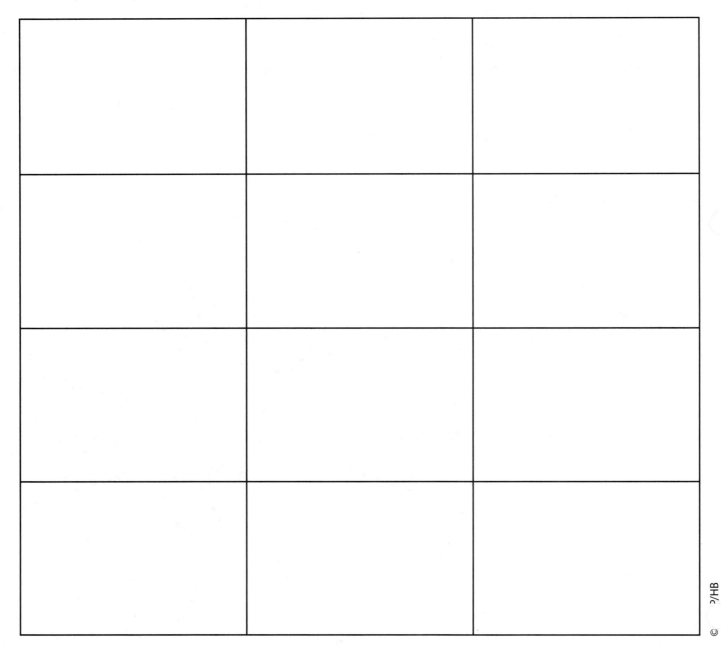

BH/c
©

Name _____ Date _____

One Well

I. All water on Earth is connected.

   A. about 70% of Earth's surface is water

   B. some water is buried deep under the ground

II. Water keeps moving through the water cycle.

   A. rises from water sources as gas or vapor

   B. _____

III. _____

   A. _____

   B. _____

IV. _____

   A. _____

   B. _____

V. _____

   A. _____

   B. _____

VI. _____

   A. _____

   B. _____

Use Practice Masters 5.7 and 5.8 to summarize "One Well."

Reread and Summarize: Outline

One Well (continued)

VII. **Distribution of water is different around the world.**

    A. _____

    B. _____

VIII. **We use water for many things.**

    A. _____

    B. _____

    C. _____

IX. _____

    A. _____

    B. _____

X. _____

    A. _____

    B. _____

    C. _____

XI. _____

    A. _____

    B. _____

Use your outline to summarize the selection to a partner.

P/HB

Fluency: Phrasing

One Well

Use this passage to practice reading with proper phrasing.

Imagine for a moment that all the water on Earth came from just one well.   15

This isn't as strange as it sounds. All water on Earth is connected, so there really   31

is just one source, one global well, from which we can draw all our water. Every ocean   48

wave, every lake, stream, and underground river, every raindrop and snowflake and   60

every bit of ice in glaciers and polar icecaps is a part of this global well.   76

Because it is all connected, how we treat the water in the well will affect every   92

species on the planet, now and for years to come.   102

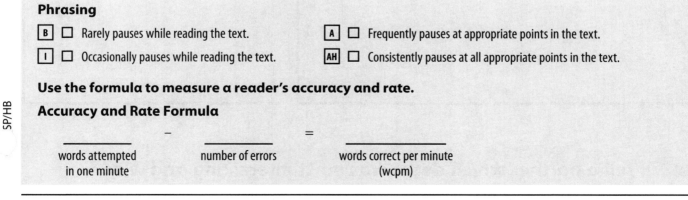

Phrasing

B ☐ Rarely pauses while reading the text.   A ☐ Frequently pauses at appropriate points in the text.

I ☐ Occasionally pauses while reading the text.   AH ☐ Consistently pauses at all appropriate points in the text.

Use the formula to measure a reader's accuracy and rate.

Accuracy and Rate Formula

_____ − _____ = _____

words attempted   number of errors   words correct per minute
in one minute   (wcpm)

Reading Options: Double-Entry Log

Picturing the Pantanal

Complete the double-entry log as you read "Picturing the Pantanal."

Page	What I read	What it reminds me of

💬 **Tell a partner which detail was most interesting and why.**

Compare Texts

	"Picturing the Pantanal"	"One Well"
Genre		
Topic		
Main Idea	Through photos, Dr. Maycira Costa studies the Pantanal, and learns how life there is affected by changes to the area.	
Text Features	Photos: _____ Tables: _____ Diagrams: _____	Photos: _____ Tables: _____ Diagrams: _____

P/HB

©

Take turns with a partner. Share what you like about both selections. Share what you like that was in only one of the selections.

Name _____   Date _____

The Pantanal

Grammar Rules Adjectives

1. Use a capital letter for adjectives that describe a country of origin.
2. Add -**er** to the adjective when you compare two things.
3. Add -**est** to the adjective to compare three or more things.
4. Some adjectives have special forms for comparing things. These include **good, better, best.**

Circle the adjectives. Underline the nouns they describe.

The Brazilian Pantanal is a strange and special place. It is the largest tropical wetland in the world. Many plants and animals live there. Heavy rain falls for months in the Pantanal. This makes the Pantanal green. It is much greener than the dry desert that Elena visited. Scientists want to learn about the amazing Pantanal. They study how human activities affect it. They believe this is the best way to protect the Pantanal for the future.

Listen as a partner tells you a noun. Use an adjective to tell about that noun. Together, make a sentence that compares that noun to another noun.

P/HB
©

Name _____   Date _____

Characters My Partner Knows

Character	Role	Function	Relationship

Use your chart to describe characters in a story your partner tells you about.

Grammar: Singular and Plural Possessives

A Science Report

Grammar Rules Singular and Plural Possessives

1. Possessive nouns tell who owns something.
   - For one owner or plural nouns not ending in **-s**, add **'s**
   - For more than one owner for nouns ending in **-s**, add only **'**
2. Possessive adjectives do **not** use apostrophes:
   - **my, your, her, his, its, our, their**

Circle the correct word.

"(Your, You, Yours) homework for tonight is to write a report about water," Mr. Lee told (her, its, his) students. One (students, student's , students') hand went up in the air.

"Can (my, its, her) report be about the canal behind my house?" asked Josh.

"(Their, My, Your) report can be anything about water," said Mr. Lee.

The next day the students all had (their, her, your) reports.

"(Me, My, I) report is about water conservation," said Ella. "I wrote about how (peoples, people's, peoples') habits at home can help save water for all of us."

Mr. Lee collected all of the (students, students', student's) reports and put them in (his, her, my) desk.

> Use possessive nouns and adjectives to tell a partner about a report you wrote.

P/HB

©

My Great-Grandmother's Gourd

1  A village got a new pump. The girl celebrated with the villagers, but her grandmother did not come. She stayed near an old baobab tree.

2 Grandmother was sad. She didn't like the new pump. She said that the villagers used to prepare the trees for the rainy season. Now she only heard the pump. The girl explained that they no longer needed to store water.

3 Grandmother prepared her tree for the rainy season. The villagers laughed. The girl helped her grandmother. Together they worked to fill the tree with water.

4 The dry season came. The pump broke. The girl and her grandmother shared their water.

The next rainy season, all the villagers prepared their trees, just in case the pump broke again.

SP & HB

Name _____   Date _____

The Make-It-Possessive Game

One Owner	Add 's.	A village's water is for everyone.
More Than One Owner	Add ' if the noun ends in -s.	The villagers' resources are important.

1. **Play with a partner.**

2. **Flip a coin. Move one space for heads. Move two spaces for tails.**

3. **Change the noun to a possessive noun. Say a sentence using the possessive noun.**

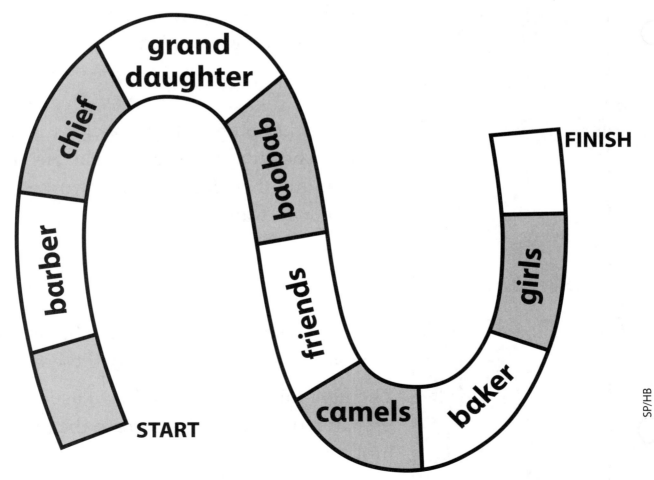

SP/HB

Name _____   Date _____

Make Your Own Game Board

1. Keep the practice going! Make your own game board.

2. In each square, write a noun that names one or more persons, animals, or things. Invite a partner to add punctuation to turn the noun into a possessive noun.

P/HB

With your partner, talk about how you changed the nouns into possessive nouns. Use the rules on Practice Master 5.16 if you need help.

Vocabulary: Apply Word Knowledge

Vocabulary Concentration

1. Write the words and definitions on index cards.

2. Lay all the cards face down. Set the words on the left and the definitions on the right.

3. Flip over one card from each side. If the word and definition match, keep the cards and try to make another match.

4. If the word and definition do not match, put the cards back.

5. Play until all the cards have been matched.

acquire	aquifer	availability	canal
capacity	channel	climate	course
distribution	gourd	region	scarcity
to get	a body of rock that can contain groundwater	the amount of something that is able to be used	a waterway made by people
the maximum amount something can hold	to bring water from one place to another	the general weather conditions in an area	the route or direction followed by water, such as a river
the way something is shared among a group	a container made by hollowing out a fleshy fruit with hard skin	an area, a part of a country	when there is not enough of something, especially a resource

P/HB ©

Name _____ Date _____

My Great-Grandmother's Gourd

Character	Role	Function	Relationship
Grandmother	grandmother		
Fatima	granddaughter		

💬 **Use your character chart to retell the story to a partner.**

© P/HB

Fluency: Expression

My Great-Grandmother's Gourd

Use this passage to practice reading with proper expression.

I looked for my grandmother, who always says she is so proud	12
of me, but I didn't see her. As people pushed forward to try the	26
pump, I pushed outward to find my grandmother.	34
There she stood all alone beneath her best friend, an old	45
baobab tree.	47
"Grandmother, come see the new pump. The water is so easy to	59
get now, our work will be less."	66
Grandmother looked at me, then patted the gnarled trunk of the	77
giant baobab tree with her work-worn hand and said, "Go child.	88
Drink the fresh, cold water. And soon I'll be there too."	99
I ran back and danced with my friends, celebrating the new	110
pump. But my grandmother did not come.	117

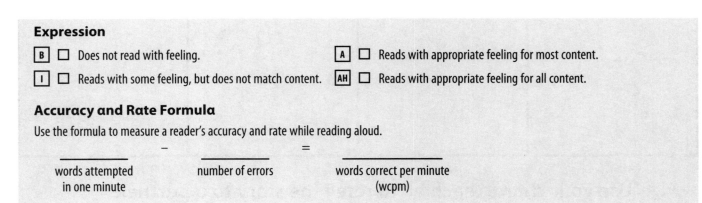

Expression

B ☐ Does not read with feeling.   A ☐ Reads with appropriate feeling for most content.

I ☐ Reads with some feeling, but does not match content.   AH ☐ Reads with appropriate feeling for all content.

Accuracy and Rate Formula

Use the formula to measure a reader's accuracy and rate while reading aloud.

_____ − _____ = _____

words attempted in one minute   number of errors   words correct per minute (wcpm)

Name _____   Date _____

Juan del Oso and the Water of Life

What I Know About Juan	What I Think Will Happen

SP/HB

💬 **Tell a partner about a prediction you had that was not exactly correct.**

Respond and Extend: Comparison Chart

Compare Themes

Themes	"Juan del Oso and the Water of Life"	"My Great-Grandmother's Gourd"
Many hands make light work.	Yes	
Work that has a purpose can benefit many.		Yes
With hard work, anything is possible.		
Don't give up old ways for new ways.		
Water is important to our lives.		
Teamwork works.		

SP/HB

💬 **Take turns with a partner giving examples from the selection to support your answers.**

Grammar: Possessive Nouns and Adjectives

The Aquifer's Future

Grammar Rules Possessive Nouns and Adjectives

1. When there is only one owner, add **'s** to show ownership.
2. When there is more than one owner and the noun ends in **-s**, just add **'** at the end of the noun.
3. When there is more than one owner and the noun does not end in **-s**, add **'s** at the end of the noun.
4. Possessive adjectives are **my, your, her, his, its, our,** and **their**.
5. Remember not to use an apostrophe with possessive adjectives.

1. Write the correct endings for possessive nouns.

2. Write possessive adjectives.

All of the town _____ citizens gathered at town hall, anxious to hear _____ mayor speak. _____ speech will be the most important she has ever made. News reporters _____ cameras were ready to film.

"We've had a severe drought this summer and the aquifer in _____ region is drying up. Each community in the region must begin _____ own water-saving policy. It is _____ proposal that we begin water rationing immediately. We must save every drop of water we can now to ensure _____ availability in the future. _____ lives depend on it!"

P/HB

ⓒ

> Write two new sentences using a possessive noun and a possessive adjective. Discuss your sentences with a partner.

Writing Project: Rubric

Development of Ideas

	Is the writing interesting and thoughtful?	**How well do you understand the ideas?**
4 Wow!	• The writer has thought about the topic carefully. • The writer states ideas clearly and develops them with many facts and examples.	• The main idea is clearly stated and easy to understand. • The details are interesting and all support the main idea.
3 Ahh.	• The writer has thought somewhat about the topic. • Most ideas are stated clearly. Some ideas are more developed than others.	• The main idea is pretty clearly stated. • Many details and facts support the main idea.
2 Hmm.	• The writer doesn't seem to have thought about the topic much. • Many ideas are not stated clearly. Few facts and examples support the writer's ideas.	• The main idea could be stated more clearly. • Only some of the details support the main idea.
1 Huh?	• The writer doesn't seem to have thought about the topic at all. • There are no facts or examples related to the topic.	• The main idea is not clear or is not stated. • Details and examples do not support a main idea.

Outline

Write the most important ideas on the lines with Roman numerals. Write the details to support each idea on the lines below the Roman numerals.

Outline

I. _____

   A. _____

   B. _____

II. _____

   A. _____

   B. _____

III. _____

   A. _____

   B. _____

Writing Project

Revise

Use the Revising Marks to revise this paragraph. Look for places to:

- **Add detail**
- **Vary sentences**

Revising Marks	
∧	Add.
℘	Take out.
⌒⟍	Move to here.

Every living thing needs water to survive. Every human needs

water to survive. Water is important? We drink water. We swim in

water. We travel by water. Water has many uses.

Edit, Proofread, and Publish

Edit and Proofread

Use the Editing Marks to edit and proofread this paragraph. Look for places to use:

- **Comparatives and Superlatives**
- **Adjectives**
- **Apostrophes**

Editing Marks	
^	Add.
℘	Take out.
⬯	Check spelling.
˅˄	Add an apostrophe.

The Pacific Ocean is huge. It's waters touch many countries. In fact, its the largest ocean on Earth. The second large is the Atlantic Ocean. The Indian Ocean is small than the Atlantic Ocean. All oceans are deep than lakes. The Great Lakes in North America are beautiful. Michigans beaches are on the west coast of Lake Michigan. It's beaches are so beautiful that they are called the United States third coast!

The Wild West

Make a concept map with the answers to the Big Question:
What does it take to settle a new land?

What does it take to settle a new land?

Name _____ Date _____

Identify Causes and Effects

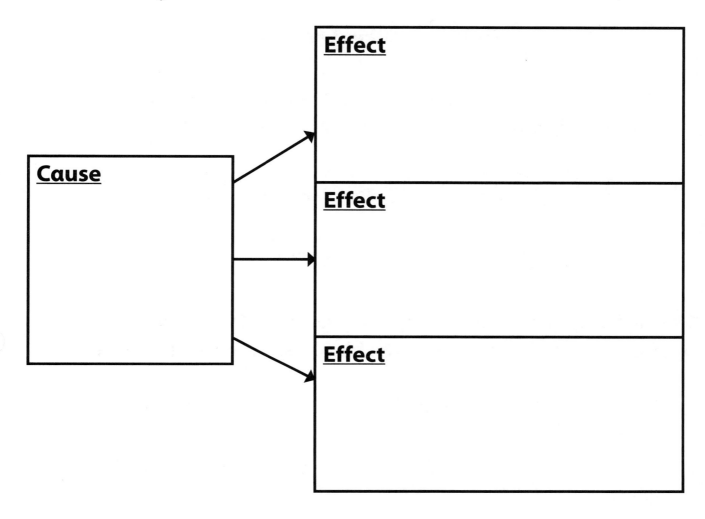

Cause

Effect

Effect

Effect

💬 **Tell your partner which effect you find most interesting and why.**

Name _____ Date _____

The Lost Calf

Grammar Rules Subject and Object Pronouns

Use subject pronouns in the subject of a sentence. Use object pronouns after the verb or a small word like *for* or *to*.

Pronouns

	One	More Than One	Contractions
Subject	I, she, he, it, you	we, you, they	I'm, you're, it's
Object	me, you, him, her, it	us, you, them	

Say each sentence. Then replace the underlined words with the correct pronoun. Write the pronoun in the blank. Say the new sentence.

1. The cowboy has a male calf. <u>The cowboy</u> guides the calf down a path. _____

2. The cowboy's wife looks for the calf. <u>The cowboy's wife</u> can't find the calf. _____

3. The cowboy and his wife are worried about the calf. <u>The cowboy and his wife</u> search for the calf. _____

4. The cowboy says, "<u>The cowboy</u> will search by the river." _____

5. The cowboy returns without the calf. He could not find <u>the calf</u>. _____

6. The cowboy's wife says, "Here he is! He returned while <u>the cowboy</u> were gone." _____

   Tell your partner something about yourself. Use the contraction *I'm*.

Name _____   Date _____

Westward Bound!

1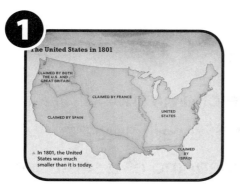

Before 1803, France, Spain, and Britain owned most of the West. Then the Louisiana Purchase was made and President Jefferson sent explorers into the West.

2

Americans first moved to the West because they wanted to own land, get rich, or find adventure.

Gold was discovered in California in 1848. People rushed West, hoping to get rich.

3

Settlers made their homes in California, Oregon, and the Midwest. They soon pushed out the Native Americans.

4

After the Civil War, cattle drives began. Cowboys took cattle from Texas to the north. The open range didn't last long, though. Soon most of the West was settled.

© P/HB

Name _____   Date _____

The Reflexive Pronoun Game

Grammar Rules Reflexive Pronouns

1. A pronoun is a word that takes the place of a noun.
2. A reflexive pronoun refers to the subject of a sentence.
3. A reflexive pronoun is necessary for the meaning of a sentence.
4. A reflexive pronoun ends in -*self* or -*selves*.
5. These are the reflexive pronouns: *myself, herself, himself, itself, ourselves, themselves.*

1. **Play with a partner.**
2. **Flip a coin. Move one space for heads. Move two spaces for tails.**
3. **Complete the sentence by saying the correct reflexive pronoun. If you are correct, flip the coin again. If you are incorrect, your partner flips the coin.**
4. **The winner is the player who reaches the finish space first.**

She asked _____ when she would feel at home in the West.	He saw _____ on the glassy surface of the water.	The cat purred _____ to sleep.		
I told _____ that the journey west would be exciting.		We enjoyed _____ during the square dance.		FINISH
START		The horses jammed _____ against the fence when they heard the loud noise.	We enjoyed _____ while husking corn.	The settlers placed _____ in the best positions to pan for gold.

P/HB

©

Vocabulary: Apply Word Knowledge

Yes or No

Think of a Key Vocabulary word. Then think of a question you can ask about its meaning. Make sure the question can be answered yes or no. Read the examples, then write two yes or no questions of your own.

1. When you explore, do you often discover new things?

2. Does construction mean taking things apart?

3. Do cowboys work in ranching?

4. Did the gold rush happen in the 1900s?

5. Were reservations created for settlers?

6. When there is expansion, are things smaller?

7. When you talk about an individual, are you talking about one person?

8. Did settlers go west to find big cities?

9. _____

10. _____

5P/HB

Name _____ Date _____

Westward Bound!

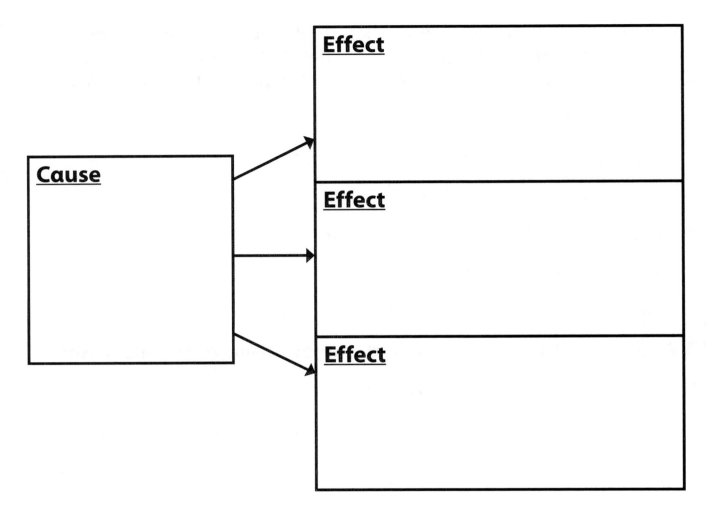

Cause

Effect

Effect

Effect

Use your organizer to retell the selection to a partner.

5P/HB

Name _____   Date _____

Use this passage to practice reading with proper intonation.

Westward Bound!

If you ask anyone about the history of the West, they may tell you about a wild,	17
lawless time, when brave cowboys rode their horses across wide, dusty plains.	29
This is a popular vision of the Old West. It is often shown on TV and in the	47
movies. But it is not the whole story.	55

The real history of the West is much more interesting. It is the story of millions	71
of different kinds of people, all with different ideas about the land and their	85
future on it. They came from many different backgrounds, but they had one	98
thing in common. They lived in a time of great changes. It was the time of the	115
westward expansion.	117

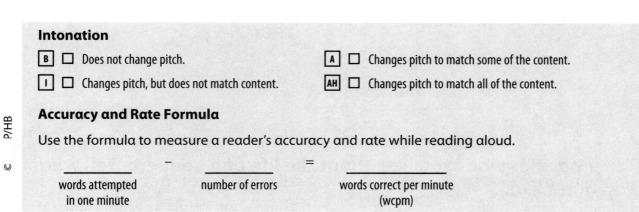

Intonation

B ☐ Does not change pitch.   A ☐ Changes pitch to match some of the content.

I ☐ Changes pitch, but does not match content.   AH ☐ Changes pitch to match all of the content.

Accuracy and Rate Formula

Use the formula to measure a reader's accuracy and rate while reading aloud.

_____ − _____ = _____
words attempted   number of errors   words correct per minute
in one minute   (wcpm)

Reading Options: Strategy Planner

A Day in the Life of a Vaquero

Step **1** What is the author's main purpose for writing?

❏ to tell a story   **OR**   ❏ to give information

❏ to entertain

Step **2** What is your purpose for reading?

❏ for enjoyment   **OR**   ❏ for information

Step **3** What type of story are you going to read?

❏ **fiction**   **OR**   ❏ **nonfiction**

Do the following:	Do the following:
• Identify the characters and settings.	• Read more slowly.
• Think about what happens and when it happens.	• Identify facts about real people or events.
	• Use maps, diagrams, and pictures.
• Use what you know to read new words.	• Concentrate as you read.

Tell a partner what you like about the life of a vaquero. Tell what you don't like.

P & HB

Name _____   Date _____

Compare Author's Purpose

	"A Day in the Life of a Vaquero"	"Westward Bound!"
What was the author's main purpose? • give information or explain • persuade readers • entertain, describe, or express personal feelings • tell how to do something		
How do you know? Give examples.		

P/HB

© ▭ Take turns with a partner. Share one question you could ask both authors. Share one question you have for only one author.

Name _____ Date _____

Lewis and Clark

Grammar Rules Pronoun Agreement

1. Use **I** or **me** to talk about yourself. Use **we** or **us** to talk about yourself and another person.

2. Use **he** or **him** for a boy or man. Use **she** or **her** for a girl or woman. Use **it** for a thing.

3. Use **they** or **them** for two or more people or things. Use **you** to talk <u>to</u> one person or more than one person.

4. Use pairs of pronouns that match in person and number to talk about a person twice in one sentence. (he, himself)

Circle the nouns. Rewrite the sentence with pronouns in place of the nouns.

1. Sacajawea helped Lewis and Clark. _____

2. Lewis and Clark asked many questions. _____

3. President Jefferson learned a lot because of Sacajawea, too. _____

4. Lewis and Clark were great teachers. _____

5. Now President Jefferson, the people, and I know a lot about the American West. _____

Have a partner choose a noun. Tell the noun's number and gender. Then pick a pronoun that can replace the noun. Together, make a sentence using a pair of pronouns with that number and gender.

Thinking Map: Cause-and-Effect Chain

The Effects of Moving

Make notes in your cause-and-effect chain as your partner tells you about a time when a friend or relative moved away.

Cause	First Effect	Second Effect

SP/HB

With your partner, talk about the move. Use your cause-and-effect chain to show what happened because of the move.

Grammar: Singular and Plural Possessive Pronouns

Our Move Out West

Grammar Rules Singular and Plural Possessive Pronouns

Possessive pronouns take the place of a person's name and what the person owns.

1. For singular possessive pronouns, use mine, yours, his, or hers.

2. For plural possessive pronouns, use ours, yours, or theirs.

Choose the correct word from the box. Write it on the blank line.

mine	yours	his	hers	ours	theirs

1. My brother gave me a book for my birthday. The book is

_____ .

2. My book tells about a family in the 1800s. The family traveled in a wagon along the Oregon Trail. The wagon was _____ .

3. The family had a father, a sister, and a brother. The sister brought a diary. The diary was _____ . She wrote about her pet dog. They had to leave the dog behind when they moved.

4. The brother brought one coat. The coat was _____ .

5. The family's journey reminds me of the time we moved to a new home. When we moved, my mother gave me a dog. "This dog is _____ now," said my mother. But I know the dog belongs to the whole family. The dog is _____ .

Use possessive pronouns to tell a partner about a time you visited a family member or took a trip somewhere.

SP/HB

The Road to Rhyolite

1 In a desert, two prospectors searched for ore. They discovered gold! They staked their claim and began to mine.

2 Word traveled fast and soon many people began to arrive. A little town named Rhyolite began to grow. People built homes, stores, banks, hotels, and a school. Soon the population grew.

3 Then financial problems struck the town. Gold became hard to find. Investors withdrew their money and mines began to close. People left the town and its buildings crumbled. Now Rhyolite is just a ghost town in the desert dust.

© P/HB

Grammar: Demonstrative and Indefinite Pronouns

What or Who Is It?

Grammar Rules Demonstrative and Indefinite Pronouns

1. A demonstrative pronoun refers to a specific noun without naming it.
2. An indefinite pronoun does not refer to a specific person or thing.

Read each sentence. Underline the demonstrative or indefinite pronoun. Draw a line from each sentence to the type of pronoun used in the sentence.

1. <u>These</u> are not valuable.
2. **Does anyone need water?**
3. That is shiny.
4. Was anything found in the mine?
5. This is gold.
6. Will somebody get rich?
7. Nobody is in the restaurant.
8. Everyone wants gold.
9. Those are small pieces.
10. That is a new hotel.

Demonstrative Pronoun

Indefinite Pronoun

© P/HB

Grammar: Demonstrative and Indefinite Pronouns

Grammar Rules Demonstrative and Indefinite Pronouns

1. Demonstrative pronouns, such as *this, that, these,* and *those* point out specific people, places, or things without naming them.
   These are boomtowns.

2. Indefinite pronouns, such as *everyone, all, someone,* and *anything,* do not tell about specific people or things.
   Soon, everyone was moving west.

Complete each sentence with an indefinite or demonstrative pronoun.

During the gold rush, many towns grew quickly. _____ changed many lives. Prospectors dug for gold all over. Where did they find it? _____ was a secret. However, _____ could stop others from finding out. It seemed as if _____ in the world was moving west to look for gold!

At first, towns became boomtowns. Usually, _____ ran out of gold. After all, _____ can dig for gold, but not _____ can find it or keep it!

Talk with a partner about the pronouns you used. Tell which are indefinite and which are demonstrative.

Name _____ Date _____

The Road to Rhyolite

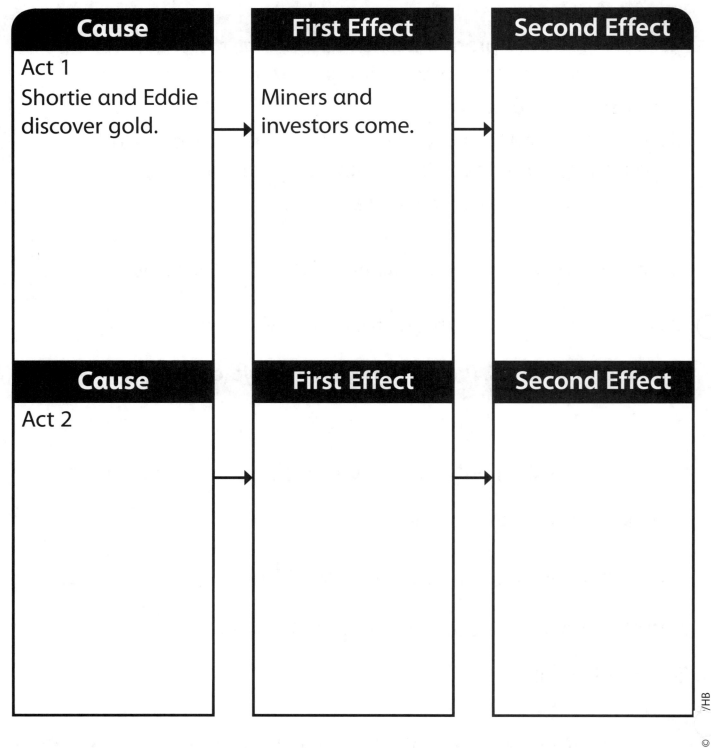

Cause	First Effect	Second Effect
Act 1 Shortie and Eddie discover gold.	Miners and investors come.	

Cause	First Effect	Second Effect
Act 2		

Use your cause-and-effect chain to retell the play to a partner.

Fluency: Expression

Use this passage to practice reading with proper expression.

The Road to Rhyolite

AGNES [*to audience*]: Well, here I am again. I know it doesn't seem   13

possible, but two years have passed since I saw you last, and things   26

are changing in Rhyolite.   30

[*Enter miners:* DOYLE, MARY, GISH, *and* YANG. *They look glum.*]   40

MARY [*angrily*]: The mines are drying up and so am I!   51

YANG: There is hardly any gold left in the ground.   61

GISH: There's only dirt and rocks and dirty socks.   70

DOYLE [*sadly*]: Looks like the good times are gone.   79

[*Enter* NEWSBOY *carrying newspapers.*]   83

NEWSBOY: Rhyolite businesses going bankrupt! Read all about it!   92

[AGNES *grabs a newspaper and reads it. Exit* NEWSBOY.]   101

Expression

B ☐ Does not read with feeling.   A ☐ Reads with appropriate feeling for most content.

I ☐ Reads with some feeling, but does not match content.   AH ☐ Reads with appropriate feeling for all content.

Accuracy and Rate Formula

Use the formula to measure a reader's accuracy and rate while reading aloud.

$$\underline{\hspace{3cm}} - \underline{\hspace{3cm}} = \underline{\hspace{3cm}}$$

words attempted   number of errors   words corrected per minute
in one minute   (wcpm)

Name _____   Date _____

Rhyolite: The True Story of a Ghost Town

Page	What I Read	What It Means to Me

Would you have enjoyed living in Rhyolite when it was a boomtown? Tell a partner why or why not.

Respond and Extend: Comparison Chart

Compare Genres

	Narrative Poem	Play
Setting		
Structure and Organization Use these words to tell about the organization and structure of the selections: • acts and scenes • dialogue • plot • rhyme • verses		

In your opinion, which selection told the more powerful story about Rhyolite? Use your chart to help. you explain your opinion.

© | & HB

Grammar: Different Kinds of Pronouns

All Aboard!

Grammar Rules Different Kinds of Pronouns

1. Possessive pronouns **mine, yours, his, hers, its, ours,** and **theirs** show who owns something and what is owned.

    We found some pickaxes. Are they <u>yours</u>?

2. Demonstrative pronouns **this, that, these,** and **those** tell about specific people, places, animals, or things without naming them.

    <u>These</u> belong to Shortie and <u>those</u> belong to Gish.

3. Indefinite pronouns **everyone, somebody, all, anybody,** and **anything** do not tell about specific people or things.

    <u>Anybody</u> can dig for gold in Rhyolite.

Complete each sentence with a possessive, an indefinite, or a demonstrative pronoun.

The train captain shouted, "All aboard _____ ! _____ is the last
                                        (indefinite)   (demonstrative)
train out of Rhyolite. We don't want to leave _____ behind."
                                               (indefinite)

Mr. Young anxiously asked his wife, "Do you have your ticket?

_____ is in my pocket. Do the children have _____ ? We must
(possessive)   (possessive)
hurry to catch _____ !"
                (demonstrative)

Write three new sentences, each using a different kind of pronoun. Share your sentences with a partner.

Writing Project: Rubric

Voice and Style

	Does the writing sound real? Is it unique to the writer?	How interesting are the words? Do they fit the purpose and the audience?
4 Wow!	• The writing shows who the writer is and sounds genuine and unique. • The writer seems to be talking to me.	• The writer uses many words that are interesting and that create sounds and pictures. • The words fit the audience and purpose well.
3 Ahh.	• For the most part, the writing sounds genuine and shows who the writer is. • The writer seems to care about the ideas in the writing.	• The writer uses some words that are interesting and that create sounds and pictures. • The words fit the audience and purpose.
2 Hmm.	• It's hard to tell who the writer is. • Only a few parts of the writing seem genuine and unique. • The writer does not seem to be talking to me.	• The writer uses a few words that are interesting or that create sounds and pictures. • Some of the words fit the audience and purpose.
1 Huh?	• I can't tell who the writer is. • The writer does not seem to care.	• The writer uses very few or no words that are interesting or that create sounds and pictures. • The words do not fit the audience and purpose.

©/HB

Cause-and-Effect Chain

Complete the cause-and-effect chain for your narrative poem.

Cause

⇩

Effect 1

⇩

Effect 2

⇩

Effect 3

⇩

Effect 4

Name _____ Date _____

Revise

Use the Revising Marks to revise this poem. Look for:

- a clear and individual voice and style
- details about characters and setting

Revising Marks

∧	Add.
℘	Take out.

Our wagon moved

On the road.

Our father said,

The wagon could carry a big load.

P/HB

Writing Project

Edit and Proofread

Use the Editing Marks to edit and proofread this narrative poem.
Look for:

- correct pronouns
- correct use of quotations and quotation marks
- words spelled correctly

Editing Marks

∧	Add.
℘	Take out.
⬭⟋	Move to here.
⬭	Check spelling.
⟩	Comma.
« »	Quotation marks

The Storm

Dad had said "Their is a storm to

come."

Still, she plodded on through mud and ice.

Should we stop the wagon or go ahead?

"Keep on going was Dad's advice.

The wind picked up. It's howl was mighty.

We waited, huddled, for the storm to cease.

By morning it could see the sun.

The storm had stopped. We were at peace.

P & HB ©

Unit Concept Map

Talking About Trash

Make a concept map with the answers to the Big Question:
Why should we care about garbage?

Thinking Map: Author's Viewpoint Chart

Author's Viewpoint

Viewpoint	Evidence	Action Needed

Share your ideas with another pair and listen to their ideas. If their ideas are different, see if you can agree on new, better ideas.

Grammar: Adverbs

The Class Project

Grammar Rules Adverbs

An adverb tells where, when, or how.

Where?	When?	How?
everywhere outside	yesterday daily	easily quickly

Circle the adverbs below. Then categorize them as *where*, *when*, or *how* adverbs.

Today we will start a project. Listen carefully for the directions. First, we will clean the classroom well. Then we will recycle plastic and paper. We will make a container for each. Please put all your bottles there and your paper here. Make sure you wash bottles thoroughly. We will empty the containers weekly.

Where?	When?	How?

Tell your partner a way you can reduce garbage. Use at least two adverbs.

P/HB

Name _____   Date _____

The World of Waste

1

Americans throw away a lot of garbage every year. Garbage is building up all over our planet. People need to think about what they buy and what they throw away.

2

Americans produce the most trash. Many other countries produce less trash because they buy less. They reuse more of what they have. Some countries even encourage people to recycle trash.

3

Leftover food and yard waste can be composted. Clothes and electronics can be donated. Jars, bottles, and toys can be reused. Plastic bottles can be recycled into play equipment.

4

You can reduce garbage. Borrow instead of buying. Remember that energy and resources are used to make trash. That's why it should be treated like treasure. Choose items with less packaging. Think of the future.

Grammar: Adverbs that Compare Action

The Comparison Adverb Game

Grammar Rules **Adverbs that Compare Actions**

1. Use a comparative adverb to compare two actions.
2. Form some comparative adverbs by adding *-er* to the adverb.
3. Use *more* or *most* with an adverb that ends in *-ly*.
4. Use a superlative adverb to compare three or more actions.
5. Form some superlative adverbs by adding *-est* to the adverb.

1. **Play with a partner.**
2. **Flip a coin. Move one space for heads, two spaces for tails.**
3. **Complete the sentence by saying the correct form of the adverb. If you are correct, flip the coin again. If you are incorrect, your partner flips the coin.**
4. **The winner is the player who reaches the finish first.**

He will arrive at the environment club meeting (soon) _____ than his friend will.	Our class recycles paper (carefully) _____ than Mr. Smith's class.	The city's landfill fills up (rapidly) _____ in the whole state.	
I add to the compost bin (quickly) _____ than you do.		Samir plans projects the (fast) _____ of all.	**FINISH**
START		Tam plans recycling the (skillfully) _____ of all.	Maria works (hard) _____ than Sue does.	You do your pollution research the (happily) _____ of all.

Name _____ Date _____

The World of Waste

Viewpoint	Evidence	Action Needed
Garbage can be good.		

Use your chart to retell the author's viewpoint and evidence to a partner. Work with your partner to find additional kinds of evidence the author uses to support her viewpoint. Add them to the evidence column.

SP & HB

Fluency: Intonation

Use this passage to practice reading with proper intonation.

The World of Waste

Americans win first prize! We produce more garbage than any 10

other country in the world. Look at the graphic at the right. It shows 24

about how much trash each person produces in one day, in different 36

countries. Compared with people in the United States, people in other 47

countries produce less trash. How is this possible? They buy fewer 58

things, and reuse and recycle more of them. 66

Some countries even encourage people to recycle. In 74

Switzerland, for example, people have to pay for every bag of garbage 86

they want taken away, but recyclable garbage is taken away for free. 98

Now that's a good reason to recycle! 105

Intonation

B ☐ Does not change pitch.   A ☐ Changes pitch to match some of the content.

I ☐ Changes pitch, but does not match content.   AH ☐ Changes pitch to match all of the content.

Accuracy and Rate Formula
Use the formula to measure a reader's accuracy and rate while reading aloud.

_____   −   _____   =   _____

words attempted   number of errors   words correct per minute
in one minute   (wcpm)

SP & HB

Reading Options: Fact Cards

Message in a Bottle

Use this page to keep track of the interesting facts you find. Use this format to set up your notes as you find more facts.

That's a fact!

An interesting fact about _____

is _____

I found it in the book _____

by _____

_____   _____
            Name   Date

That's a fact!

An interesting fact about _____

is _____

I found it in the book _____

by _____

_____   _____
            Name   Date

Tell a partner which fact surprised you the most and why.

Name _____ Date _____

Compare Author's Purpose

	"The World of Waste"	"Message in a Bottle"
Tell the author's main purpose for each selection.		
List three conclusions about each selection.		
Say how well each author's purpose was achieved.		

Think of a book you like. Tell a partner what the author's purpose was for writing and how you know.

Grammar: Adverbs

Describe It Better

Grammar Rules Adverbs

1. Use an adverb to describe a verb.
2. Use an adverb to tell how often something happens.
3. Use an adverb to describe an adjective or another adverb.

Add an adverb from the list below to tell more about an adverb, adjective, or verb in each sentence. Write the new sentence on the line.

| very | weekly | carefully | always |

1. Some communities are creative about recycling. _____

_____

2. People collect cans and take them for recycling. _____

_____

3. They clean the empty cans so they are safe. _____

_____

4. Some people bring their own bags when they shop. _____

_____

Tell a partner another creative way to recycle. Use at least one adverb in your sentence.

P & HB

Name _____ Date _____

A Goal-and-Outcome Story

Somebody (character(s))	Wanted (goal)	But (obstacle(s))	So (outcome)

P/HB

Work with a partner to tell about goals, obstacles, and outcomes in a story you have read recently.

Grammar: Prepositions

Trash Day

Grammar Rules Prepositions

A preposition is a connecting word in a phrase that can tell where, show direction, or show time.

- prepositions that tell where: **in, on, over, by, near**
- prepositions that show direction: **to, into, around, across, down, through**
- prepositions that show time: **before, during, after**

Choose prepositions from the box below to correctly fill in each blank.

after	by	during	before	in	down	over	near

My family makes an effort to dispose of their garbage _____

the day. We do not like to put the trash cans out _____ dark.

Twice each week _____ breakfast, the garbage truck comes

_____ my house. The workers pick up our trash and drive

_____ the block. They dispose of the trash _____ the landfill.

The landfill is _____ the bridge _____ the end of town.

Tell a partner where and when you might pick up litter. Have your partner name the prepositions you used.

Name _____   Date _____

Where I Live

1

Elena is writing a report about garbage. From her window she can see kids littering. She wonders if the kids know about recycling.

2

Elena goes to the store with the reusable shopping bag. Her friend Ricky goes with her. The grocer gives them gum. Ricky throws his wrapper on the ground. Angrily, Elena picks it up. Later, outside her apartment building, she starts counting the pieces of gum stuck to her steps.

3

Elena goes home to finish her report. She thinks of all the gum and trash on her street. She knows most of it could be recycled. She imagines using compost in a flower box to brighten the environment.

© P/HB

Grammar: Prepositional Phrases

Preposition Story

Grammar Rules

1. A prepositional phrase starts with a preposition and ends with a noun or pronoun.

2. The noun or pronoun is the object of the preposition.

1. Copy these words onto index cards. Lay them out face down.
2. Divide the cards evenly between you and your partner.
3. Tell a story about a piece of garbage on a journey.
4. The player who uses all of his or her cards wins!

in front of	over	under	between
on	beside	across	over
next to	into	through	around
off	against	toward	in

Tell a partner where you put garbage. Have your partner name the prepositional phrases in your sentences.

P/HB

Where I Live

Somebody (Characters)	Wanted (Goal)	But (Obstacle(s))	So (Outcome)
Elena			

Work with a partner. Tell what clues you used to figure out Elena's goals and obstacles. Then work together to talk about Ricky's goals and obstacles. Add them to your chart.

© & HB

Name _____ Date _____

"Where I Live"

Intonation is the rise and fall in the pitch or tone of your voice as you read aloud. Use this passage to practice reading with proper intonation.

"Hey," I call to Ricky, who is now by himself. Where did Pablo 12

What's-His-Name go? Maybe his mother called him—mothers are 23

always yelling from open windows, "*¡Venaca!* It's time to eat!" 33

Ricky, whose shoelaces are undone, joins me, the marbles 42

clicking in his pocket with each step. 49

You're probably thinking, do I LIKE Ricky? No. He's smaller 59

than me, only seven years old, and likes marbles and his army men. 72

Also, if he were to show you his knees, you would see that they have 87

scabs the color of bacon. I don't have scabs, and unlike Ricky, who 100

always has *mocos* sliding out of his nostrils, I almost never catch colds. And if I 114

do, I use tissue and dispose of it properly. 123

From "Where I Live," page 507

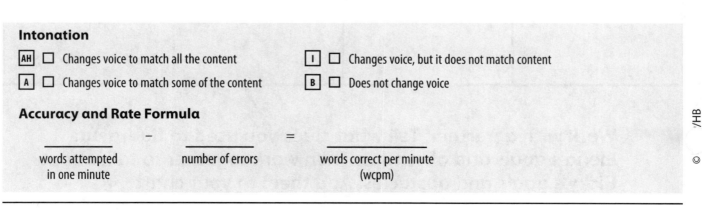

Intonation

| AH | ☐ Changes voice to match all the content | | I | ☐ Changes voice, but it does not match content |
| A | ☐ Changes voice to match some of the content | | B | ☐ Does not change voice |

Accuracy and Rate Formula

| _____ | − | _____ | = | _____ |
| words attempted in one minute | | number of errors | | words correct per minute (wcpm) |

Name _____ Date _____

Alike and Different!

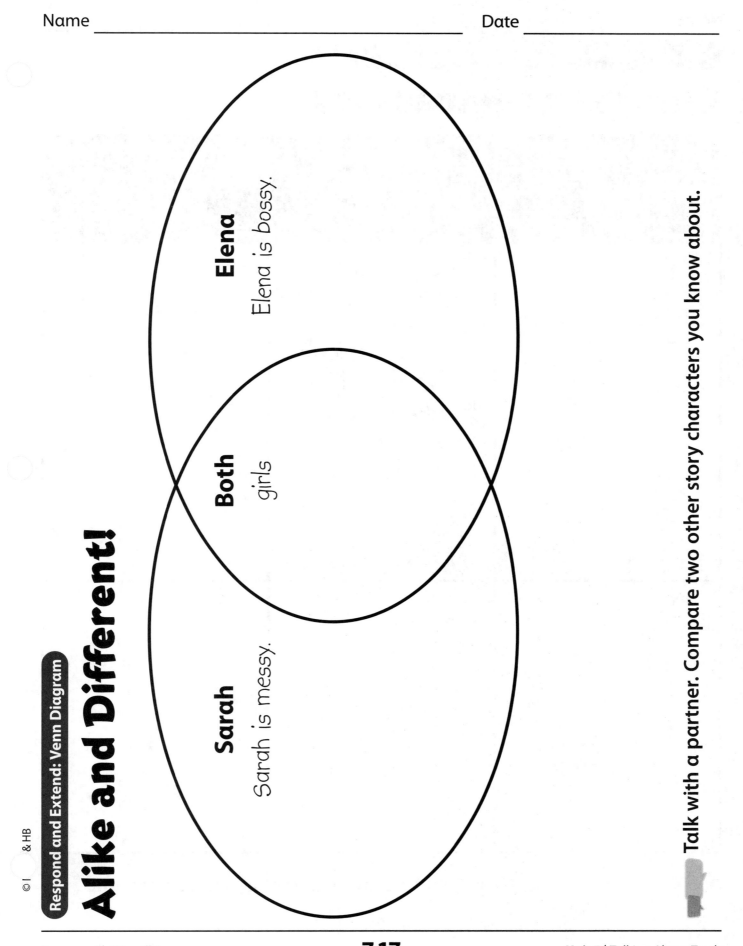

Sarah

Sarah is messy.

Both

girls

Elena

Elena is bossy.

Talk with a partner. Compare two other story characters you know about.

Compare Characters

Character	What the Character Does	What This Shows About the Character
Elena	She gets angry when she sees waste on the street. She tells people to pick up their litter. She dreams about choosing an ice-cream flavor. She dreams about a flower box with beautiful flowers.	She is bossy.
Sarah		

💬 **Talk with a partner. Compare two other story characters you know about.**

7.18

/HB

Grammar: Prepositional Phrases

Ricky's Story

Grammar Rules Prepositional Phrases

1. Use prepositional phrases to show location:
Ricky played <u>near Elena's apartment</u>.

2. Use prepositional phrases to show direction:
Elena and Ricky headed <u>down the street</u>.

3. Use prepositional phrases to show time:
<u>After school</u>, Ricky plays marbles with his cousin Pablo.

4. Use prepositional phrases to give details:
Elena wrote a report <u>about recycling</u>.

Write prepositional phrases.

   My name is Ricky, and I live _____ as Elena.
I play marbles _____ after school every day. One day
_____, Elena asked me to go with her _____ to buy
eggs and milk. When we saw the ice cream treats _____, we
dreamed _____. When Elena paid for the eggs and milk,
Mr. Asmara gave us some gum. Elena yelled at me when I threw
the gum wrapper _____. She taught me an important
lesson: Don't litter!

Tell a partner about places where you can find litter. Use prepositional phrases in your sentences.

"Elena's War on Trash"

Setting: The play takes place in Elena's neighborhood, at a store and at her apartment.

Cast of Characters: Narrator, Elena, Ricky, Mr. Asmara

Scene 1: On Elena's Street

Elena and Ricky are walking down the sidewalk in their neighborhood. There is a lot of trash on the ground. Elena looks grumpy. Ricky isn't paying attention.

Narrator: Elena is writing a report on the environment. Everywhere she looks in her neighborhood, she sees people who are littering. It drives her crazy!

Elena *[angrily]*: I can't believe that people just throw this trash on the ground!

Ricky *[daydreaming]*: Huh?

Elena: I said, look at all this trash! Come on, let's go to the store. I have to get eggs and milk for Mom.

Ricky: OK, Elena.

Scene 2: At the store

Elena and Ricky stand in front of a freezer. They're looking at a lot of different ice cream bars.

Ricky: Mmmm. Those ice cream bars look good!

Elena: Yeah, they do. I wish we had enough money to buy some. What would you get?

Ricky: An ice cream sandwich!

Elena: I'd like an orange one… *[looking into the store]* Hi, Mr. Asmara. May I have some eggs and milk, please?

Mr. Asmara: Here you go, Elena. And here's a little treat for you and Ricky.

Mr. Asmara hands eggs and milk to Elena. There are two small boxes of gum on top of the egg carton. Elena carefully puts the eggs and milk into a canvas shopping bag.

Ricky and Elena: Thanks, Mr. Asmara!

Ricky and Elena unwrap their gum and put it in their mouths. Elena puts her gum wrapper in her pocket, but Ricky drops his on the ground.

Elena *[furious]*: What did you just do? We shouldn't litter! Come on, let's go home.

Ricky *[ashamed]*: I'm sorry, Elena.

Elena bends to pick up the wrapper, and puts it in her pocket. She and Ricky walk offstage.

Scene 3: In Elena's kitchen

Elena puts the milk and eggs in the fridge. She grumbles to herself as she puts the gum wrappers in the trash can.

Elena: There's so much trash out there! This neighborhood is drowning in it! But what can I do? I'm only a fifth grader. Nobody listens to me.

Elena sits at the kitchen table. She begins writing her report again.

Narrator: Elena thought hard. She didn't want much—just a pretty place to live, without all the trash. She remembered some pictures she had seen in a calendar. They showed all kinds of beautiful scenes—a frozen river, bright yellow daffodils, and a surfer riding a wave. Finally, she got an idea.

Elena: I know! I'll make my own pretty place right here! I can plant a flowerbox. I'm sure that birds, bees, and butterflies will come to visit all the flowers. Now that would be just like a calendar!

End of play

Writing Project: Rubric

Development of Ideas

	Is the writing interesting and unusual?	How well are the ideas presented?
4 Wow!	• The writer has thought about the topic very carefully. • The ideas are presented in a very interesting way.	• The writer's opinion is very clearly stated. • The writing uses good, clear reasons and details to support the opinion.
3 Ahh.	• The writer has thought about the topic. • The ideas are presented in an interesting way.	• The writer's opinion is clearly stated. • The writing uses reasons and details to support the opinion.
2 Hmm.	• The writer doesn't seem to have thought about the topic very much. • The writing is OK, but not interesting.	• The writer's opinion is not exactly clear. • Only one or two reasons are given to support the opinion.
1 Huh?	• The writer doesn't seem to have thought about the topic at all. • The ideas are presented in a boring way.	• The writer doesn't seem to have an opinion. • No evidence is given.

Author's Viewpoint Chart

Complete the author's viewpoint chart for your persuasive essay.

Viewpoint	Evidence	Action Needed

Writing Project: Revise

Revise

Use the Revising Marks to revise these paragraphs. Look for:

- a clearly stated opinion
- reasons, facts, and examples that support the opinion
- a clear statement about the action people should take.

Revising Marks	
∧	Add.
℘	Take out.

Water to Survive

Every living thing needs water to survive. Every human needs water to survive.

Water is important. When the quality of water changes, it changes the health of living things. We should do many things to help with water on Earth. Everyone can do something.

Writing Project: Edit

Edit and Proofread

Use the Editing Marks to edit and proofread this paragraph. Look for:

- **correct spelling of adverbs**
- **correct use of adverbs**
- **correct use of semi-colons and colons.**

Editing Marks	
∧	Add.
℘	Take out.
⬭	Check spelling.
≡	Capitalize.
ᵔ	Add an apostrophe.

Let's reuse old wood and other materials for our gardens! Every

Saturday, I go with my uncle to look for things people no longer

want. We oftener pick up pieces of wood and old windows we

can easyly use these to build a greenhouse. We also sometimesly

find these items cardboard, paper, bins, and boxes. We use these

materials for soil. We clean out garages and find all kinds of cool

things. I real love using old things to make new things!

SP/HB

Unit Concept Map

One Idea

Make a concept map with the answers to the Big Question:
How can one idea change your future?

Tell Steps in a Process

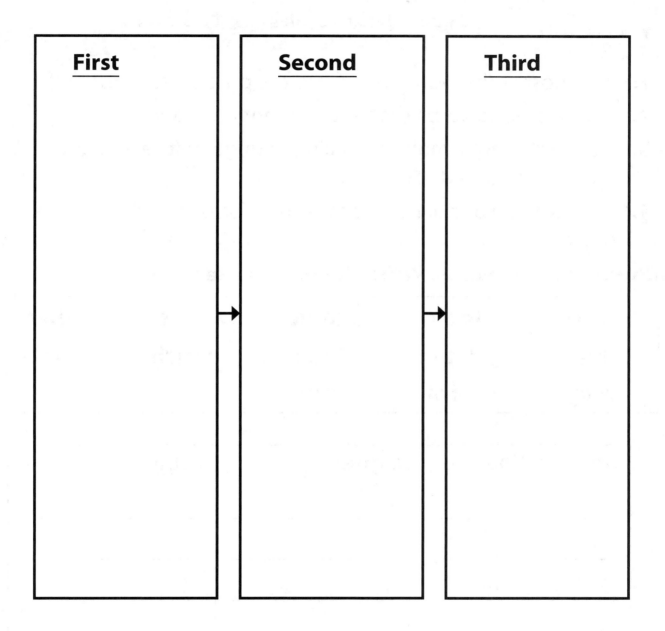

First

Second

Third

Use a sequence chain to tell a partner the steps that you would take to start a business. Use the words *first*, *second*, and *third* to explain the steps in an order that makes sense.

Grammar: Regular and Irregular Past Tense Verbs

It Happened Yesterday

Grammar Rules Regular and Irregular Past Tense Verbs

1. For most verbs, add *-ed* to form the past tense. (ordered)
2. Add just *-d* to verbs that end in silent *e*. (baked)
3. For some verbs, make a spelling change before you add *-ed*. (plan → planned; try → tried)
4. Remember special past-tense forms for *is, are, do, go, take*.

Categorize the verbs. Write the past-tense verb.

do	look	cook	save	give
fry	like	take	touch	taste
play	form	dry	go	is

Spelling Change	Regular	Irregular
_____	*cooked*	_____
_____	_____	_____
_____	_____	_____
_____	_____	_____
_____	_____	_____

Use three of the verbs above. Tell your partner something you did last week.

Grammar: Past-Tense Verbs

We Took Steps to Success!

Grammar Rules Past-Tense Verbs

1. Add just –d to verbs that end in silent e. (bake ➞ baked)
2. Double the final consonant for verbs that end in vowel + consonant (plan ➞ planned)
3. Change y to i and add –ed for verbs that end in consonant + y. (try ➞ tried)

Rewrite each sentence changing the verb to the past tense.

1. We have ideas for new businesses. _____

2. We list all the ideas on paper. _____

3. Soon, we decide which idea is best. _____
    _____

4. Everyone is excited! _____

5. We hurry to the computer. _____

6. Step by step, we follow a process. _____
    _____

7. As a result, we succeed in business! _____
    _____

8. We are proud. _____

Talk with your partner about the steps you followed to change present-tense verbs to past-tense verbs.

P/HB

Name _____   Date _____

Starting Your Own Business: Seven Steps to Success

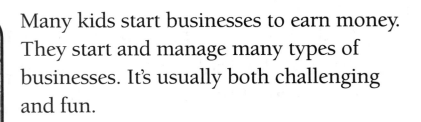

Many kids start businesses to earn money. They start and manage many types of businesses. It's usually both challenging and fun.

To start your own business, first make a plan. Decide what type of business to run. List the materials you need and determine your start-up costs. Raise your start-up money. Price your goods and services, then advertise your new business.

It is important to keep track of your income and expenses. You should also figure your profit. Have an adult check your work to be sure everything is correct.

Grammar: Present Perfect Tense

The Present Perfect Tense Game

Grammar Rules Present Perfect Tense

1. A present perfect verb tells about an action that happened at an indefinite time in the past and may still be happening.

2. Form a present perfect verb with a present tense form of *have* and the past participle.

3. A past participle usually ends in *-ed,* but there are some irregular past participles.

1. **Play with a partner.**

2. **Spin the spinner.**

3. **Read the sentence. Fill in the blank with the correct present perfect verb.**

Make a Spinner

1. Put a paper clip ⌷ in the center of the circle.

2. Hold one end of the paper clip with a pencil.

3. Spin the paper clip around the pencil.

Pat (want) _____ to start a business for a long time.

He (count) _____ the profits every week.

Maria and Dave (start) _____ a new yard business.

Lee (warn) _____ against starting a business too quickly.

She (call) _____ about the business every day.

We (fix) _____ the expenses to make them work.

They (attach) _____ the earnings sheet to the expenses sheet.

I (wonder) _____ how to make a profit.

©/HB

Starting Your Own Business

How to Plan Your Business

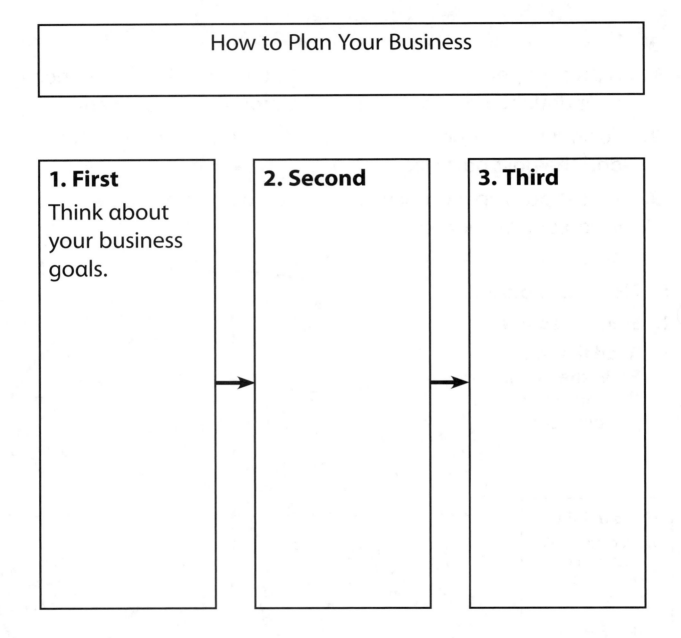

1. First	**2. Second**	**3. Third**
Think about your business goals.		

Use your organizer to explain the procedure to a partner.

Name _____   Date _____

Use this passage to practice reading with proper phrasing.

Starting Your Own Business

Have you ever dreamed of having lots of money of your own?	12
Then you should think about starting a business. Every year, thousands	23
of kids start businesses. They earn extra money to spend or to save.	36
Some kids use their business earnings to pay for trips, lessons, or	48
for college later on. Kids do more than just babysit or mow laws.	61
Many kids have found ways to make their businesses different	71
and special.	73
People who start and manage their own businesses are	82
entrepreneurs. Entrepreneurs are good planners and organizers.	89
Before starting a business, an entrepreneur finds a need and thinks	100
about how to fill it. Starting a business isn't always easy, but it's usually	114
challenging and fun.	117

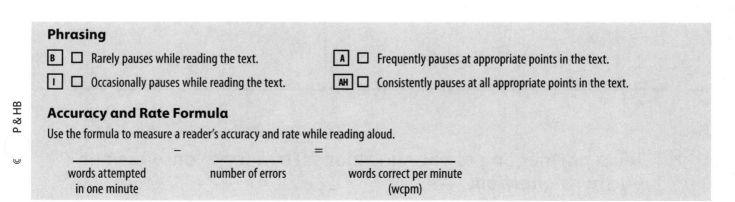

Phrasing

B ☐ Rarely pauses while reading the text.   A ☐ Frequently pauses at appropriate points in the text.

I ☐ Occasionally pauses while reading the text.   AH ☐ Consistently pauses at all appropriate points in the text.

Accuracy and Rate Formula

Use the formula to measure a reader's accuracy and rate while reading aloud.

_____ − _____ = _____
words attempted   number of errors   words correct per minute
in one minute   (wcpm)

P & HB

©

Name _____ Date _____

Questions About a Business

Page	My question	The answer

Tell a partner one of your questions. Then try to answer your partner's question.

P & HB

Compare Procedures

Steps in "Starting Your Own Business"	Steps Kayla Legare Used
1. Plan your business	✓
2.	
3.	
4.	
5.	
6.	
7.	

© ▬▬▬▬ **Take turns with a partner. Share one way Kayla could have completed one of the steps that isn't checked.**

Grammar Rules: Regular and Irregular Past-Tense Verbs

Kayla's Menus

Grammar Rules Regular/Irregular Past-Tense Verbs

1. For most verbs, add *-ed* to form the past tense (ordered).
2. Add just *-d* to verbs that end in silent *e*. (baked)
3. Double the final consonant for verbs that end in vowel + consonant (fanned).
4. Change *y* to *i* and add *-ed* for verbs that end with consonant + *y* (tried).
5. Remember special past-tense forms for *is, are, do, go, take.*

Write the past tense of the verb.

Kayla _____ special software to make menus for blind and
　　　　 (use)

visually impaired people. She _____ her business with her uncle.
　　　　　　　　　　　　　　　 (plan)

He _____ interested and wanted to help her. They _____ to
　　 (is)　　　　　　　　　　　　　　　　　　　　　　 (go)

talk to restaurant owners. Kayla _____ that no one would buy
　　　　　　　　　　　　　　　 (worry)

her menus. She and her uncle _____ happy that restaurants
　　　　　　　　　　　　　　 (are)

bought the menus.

Listen when a partner tells you a verb. Tell the past tense of the verb. Tell the spelling rules to make the past tense.

NGL/HB
©

Name _____   Date _____

Story Map

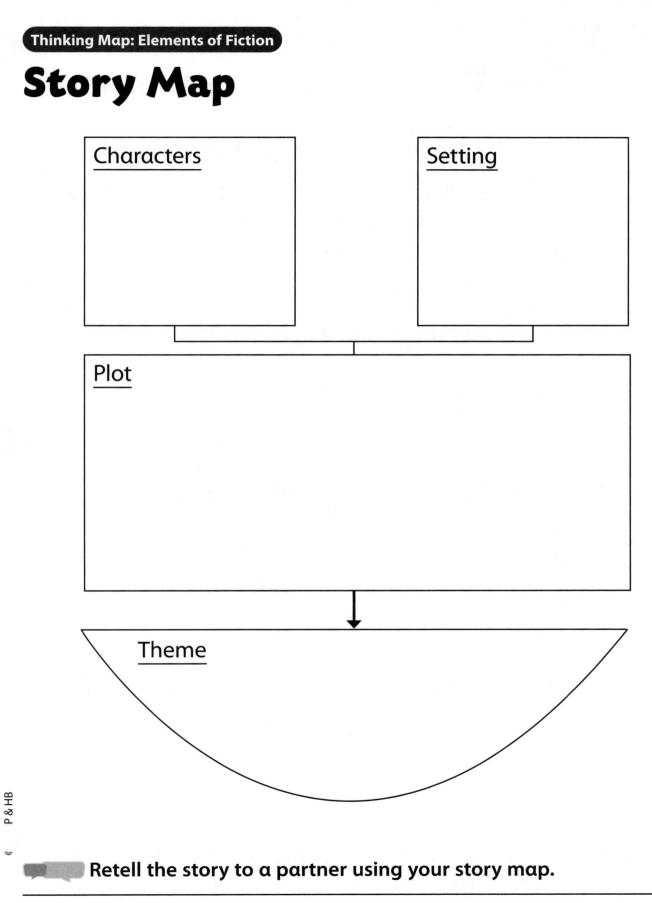

Characters

Setting

Plot

Theme

💬 **Retell the story to a partner using your story map.**

P & HB

Grammar: Past Progressive

At the Bank

Grammar Rules Past Progressive

The past progressive tells about an action that was happening over a period of time in the past. To form the past progressive:

- use helping verbs *was, were*
- add *-ing* to the main verb

Write the past–progressive form of the verb shown below each line.

1. An entrepreneur _____ for a loan from the bank.
   (ask)

2. The bank teller _____ out the paper work.
   (fill)

3. Another entrepreneur _____ money for a new business.
   (borrow)

4. Many other customers _____ in line.
   (standing)

5. They _____ to get credit from the bank, too.
   (wait)

6. They _____ about their new ideas.
   (think)

7. Across the country, new businesses _____ every day.
   (start)

8. Customers _____ new goods and services.
   (buy)

💬 **Use the past progressive to tell a partner about what you did when you had a good idea.**

P/HB
©

Key Points Reading

One Hen

1  Kojo and his mother are poor. Kojo quits school to help his mother sell wood. They borrow money and buy a cart to carry the wood. Kojo uses some of the money to buy a hen.

2  Kojo and his mother eat some of the eggs and sell the rest. They earn enough money to pay back the loan. Soon, Kojo has enough money to buy more hens. He can go back to school.

3  Kojo works hard in school. He learns more about farming. He wants to start his own farm, so he gets a loan from a bank.

Many people earn money by working on his farm. Kojo gives loans to people. He asks them to loan money to other people.

4  As people help each other, many lives improve. Kojo helps his family, his community, and his country with one good idea and a small loan.

Name _____   Date _____

The Make-It-Perfect Game

Grammar Rules Past Perfect and Present Perfect

1. The present–perfect tense describes action that began in the past yet may continue. It uses the helping verbs **have** and **has**.

2. The past–perfect tense tells about an action that was completed before some other action in the past. It uses the helping verb **had**.

applied	gone	hired	started	sold	built
helped					agreed
bought					traveled
worked					carried
used					grown
wanted					borrowed
BEGIN		**END**	succeeded	loaned	changed

1. Play with a partner.
2. Flip a coin. Move 1 space for heads. Move 2 spaces for tails.
3. Say a sentence about "One Hen" using the past-perfect or present-perfect form of the verb. If you use the verb correctly, flip the coin again.
4. To win, reach the end first!

P/HB

Read and Retell: Story Map

One Hen

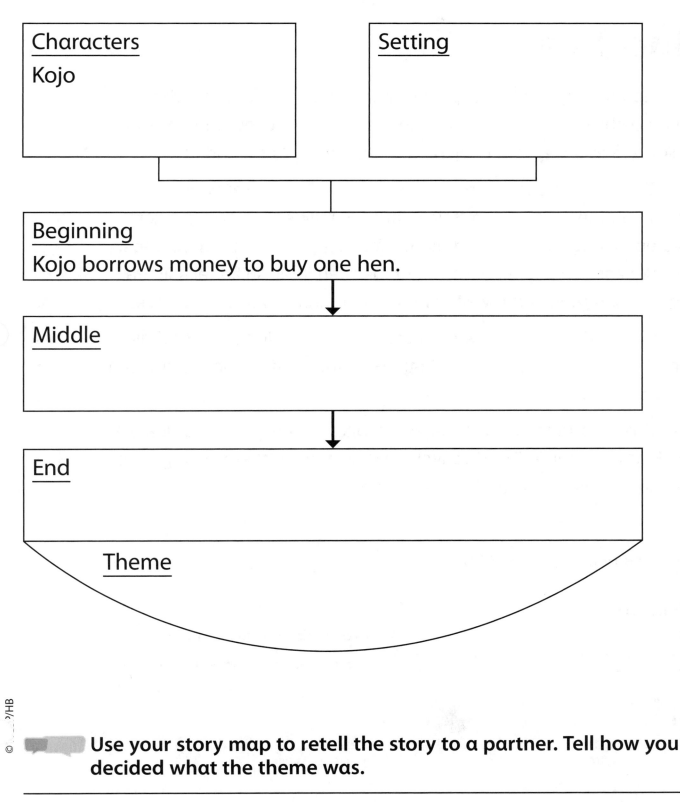

Characters
Kojo

Setting

Beginning
Kojo borrows money to buy one hen.

Middle

End

Theme

💬 **Use your story map to retell the story to a partner. Tell how you decided what the theme was.**

Fluency: Expression

Use this passage to practice reading with proper expression.

One Hen

Before long, many people are working on Kojo's farm. Men   10
feed the chickens and clean the coops. Women collect the eggs and   22
pack them in boxes. Other workers drive the eggs to markets.   33

The workers have families. One hundred and twenty people   42
depend on the wages from Kojo's farm. Families like the Odonkors   53
have enough food to eat and money for their children's school fees.   65
Ma Odonkor can buy medicine when her daughter Adika falls ill. Pa   77
Odonkor can rebuild the walls of their mud home with cinderblocks.   88

The workers on Kojo's farm can even afford livestock of their   99
own. Some families buy a goat, others a sheep, and some start with   112
one brown hen.   115

Kojo's farm is now the largest in Ghana. One day, Kojo hears a   128
knock at the door. Adika Odonkor, all grown up, is there. She greets   141
Kojo and holds out a small sack of coins.   150

From "One Hen," pages 586-587

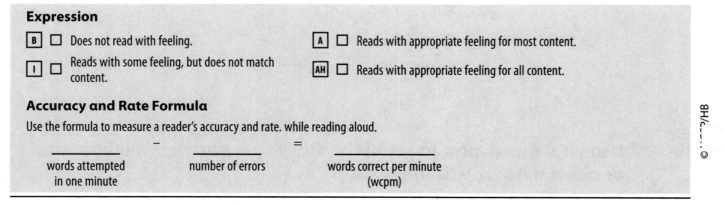

Expression

| B | ☐ Does not read with feeling. | A | ☐ Reads with appropriate feeling for most content. |

| I | ☐ Reads with some feeling, but does not match content. | AH | ☐ Reads with appropriate feeling for all content. |

Accuracy and Rate Formula

Use the formula to measure a reader's accuracy and rate. while reading aloud.

_____ − _____ = _____
words attempted   number of errors   words correct per minute
in one minute   (wcpm)

Reading Options: Strategy Planner

Strategy Planner

Step **1** What is the author's main purpose for writing this

magazine article?

❏ to tell a story   **OR**   ❏ to give information

❏ to entertain

Step **2** What is your main purpose for reading?

❏ for enjoyment   **OR**   ❏ for information

Step **3** What type of selection are you going to read?

❏ **fiction**   **OR**   ❏ **nonfiction**

Do the following:
- Identify the characters and settings.
- Think about what happens and when it happens.

Do the following:
- Identify the topic.
- Study maps and pictures.
- Read labels.

Predict what this selection will be about. After reading, confirm or revise your prediction with you partner.

P & HB

Compare Texts

	"Another Way of Doing Business"	"One Hen"
Name the businesses.		Hens and eggs
Who started it?		Kojo
Where did the start-up costs come from?	A small-business loan	
Name the start-up materials.		
Do you think it will continue to be successful? Why?		

Talk with a partner about ways businesses can help people.

Grammar: Future-Tense Verbs

Ana's Dream

Grammar Rules Future-Tense Verbs

1. Use **will + main verb** to tell about the future.
   I <u>will go</u> to market in the morning. She <u>will go</u> with me.

2. Use **to be + going to + main verb** to tell about the future.
   I <u>am going to buy</u> firewood. She <u>is going to buy</u> tools.

Write future-tense verbs. Use both rules.

Ana was tired of her job. Her dream was to be her own boss. Ana

thought to herself, "Tomorrow, I _____ to the bank and ask for a
                                    (Rule 1: go)

loan. I _____ my own business. I _____ a learning
          (Rule 2: start)   (Rule 1: open)

center for young children.

At first, the banker did not want to give Ana a loan, but Ana said,

"I _____ hard and you _____ that I _____ my
   (Rule 1: work)   (Rule 1: find)   (Rule 2: repay)

loan quickly. The banker knew that Ana would keep her word.

"You _____ your loan," he said. "Together, we _____
       (Rule 1: get)   (Rule 2: make)

sure your business succeeds."

> **Tell a partner what you would like to do for work when you are older. Use both rules in your sentences.**

& HB

Writing Project: Rubric

Voice and Style

	Does the writing sound real? Is it unique to the writer?	How interesting are the words? Do they fit the audience and purpose?
4 Wow!	• The writing shows who the writer is. • The writer seems to be talking to me.	• The writer uses many words that are interesting and persuasive. • The words really fit the audience and purpose.
3 Ahh.	• The writing shows who the writer is. • The writer seems to care about the ideas in the writing.	• The writer uses some words that are interesting and persuasive. • The words fit the audience and purpose.
2 Hmm.	• It's hard to tell who the writer is. • The writer does not seem to be talking to me.	• The writer uses a few words that are interesting or persuasive. • Some of the words fit the audience and purpose.
1 Huh?	• I can't tell who the writer is. • The writer does not seem to care.	• The writer uses a few or no words that are interesting or persuasive. • The words do not fit the audience and purpose.

Name _____   Date _____

Sequence Chain

Complete the Sequence Chain for your procedure.

Procedure Name: _____

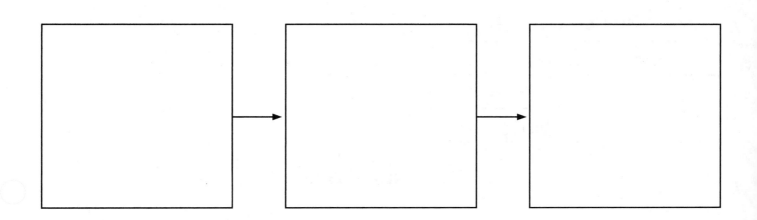

Writing Project: Revise

Revise

Use the Revising Marks to revise these paragraphs. Look for:

- **a clear statement of the procedure**
- **logical order of steps**
- **strong voice.**

Revising Marks

∧	Add.
℘	Take out.
⬭⟋	Move to here.

Clothing Drive

You can get rid of old clothes. Here's what to do.

First locate and call the used clothing drop off center in your city. Finally, take the old clothes you find to the drop-off center. Look in your home for old clothes.

By following this procedure, we can help other people in our city.

Try it.

P & HB

Edit and Proofread

Use the Editing Marks to edit and proofread these paragraphs.
Look for:

- **correct use of future tense**
- **correct use of commas with introductory words and phrases**
- **correct use of irregular verb forms.**

Editing Marks	
∧	Add.
⌄,	Add comma.
℘	Take out.

Let's ask our local city government about the coins in the fountains! We can sponsor an event to collect money for a charity. First we choose a charity to donate the money to. After that we can write a plan. Next, we can send our plan to a radio station.

We hope citizens going to throw their coins in the fountain for a good cause. Last week we do all our work getting ready for the project.

On the day of the event we can take pictures of people throwing coins into the fountain. We very excited to gather the coins and show people helping out our community.

Acknowledgments

Acknowledgments
Grateful acknowledgment is given to the authors, artists, photographers, museums, publishers, and agents for permission to reprint copyrighted material. Every effort has been made to secure the appropriate permission. If any omissions have been made or if corrections are required, please contact the Publisher.

Children's Book Press: From *My Diary from Here to There*. Copyright © 2002 by Amada Irma Perez. Illustrations © 2002 by Maya Christina Gonzales. Reprinted with permission of the publisher, Children's Book Press, San Francisco, Calif., www.childrensbookpress.org.

National Geographic Books: From *God Grew Tired of Us* by John Bul Dau with Mike Sweeney. Copyright © 2007 John Bul Dau. Reprinted by permission of the National Geographic Society. All rights reserved.

Boyd Mills Press: From *Coyote and Badger: Desert Hunters of the Southwest* by Bruce Hiscock. Text and photographs copyright © 2001 by Bruce Hiscock. Published by Caroline House, an imprint of Boyd Mills Press, Inc. Reprinted with the permission of Boyd Mills Press, Inc.

Cinco Puntos Press: From *Crossing Bok Chitto* by Tim Tingle. Copyright © 2006 by Tim Tingle. Illustrations © 2006 by Jeanne Rorex Bridges. Used with permission of Cinco Puntos Press, www.cincopuntos.com. All rights reserved.

Houghton Mifflin Harcourt: From *Harvesting Hope: The Story of Cesar Chavez* by Kathleen Krull, illustrated by Yuri Morales. Text copyright © 2003 by Kathleen Krull. Illustrations © 2003 by Yuri Morales. Used by permission of Houghton Mifflin Harcourt Publishing Company. All rights reserved.

Curtis Brown, Ltd. and Walter Lyon Krudop: From "My Great-Grandmother's Gourd" by Christina Kessler, illustrated by Walter Lyon Krudop. Text copyright © 2000 by Christina Kessler. Illustrations © 2000 by Walter Lyon Krudop. Reprinted by permission. All rights reserved.

Kids Can Press: From *One Hen: How One Small Loan Made a Big Difference* by Katie Smith Milway. Text © 2008 Katie Smith Milway. Illustrations © 2008 by Eugenie Fernandes. Reprinted by permission of Kids Can Press Ltd., Toronto.

Photographs
1.1 pocketgallery/Shutterstock. **1.14** (t) Joachim Ladefoged/VII Photo Agency, (m) Jorn Stjerneklar/Impact/HIP/The Image Works, Inc., (b) John Bul Dau. **2.13** (t) Thomas Culhane, (ml) Tatiana Popova/Shutterstock, (mr) Robert Harbison/ ©2001 The Christian Science Monitor (www.CSMonitor.com) Christian Science Monitor Publishing Society. **3.1** (b) Manfred Kage/Peter Arnold, Inc., (bx) Proland Burke/Peternold, Inc., (c, tc) Corel, (t) foloE/iStockphoto. **3.14** (1) Brett Hobson. **5.4** (1) Stockbyte/Getty Images, (4) Thomas J. Abercrombie/National Geographic Image Collection. **6.4** (2) Hulton Archive/Getty Images, (4) Library of Congress, Prints and Photographs Division Washington, D.C. 20540 USA, Reproduction No. KC-DIG-ppmsca-8790. **7.1** High Impact Photography/Shutterstock. **7.4** (3) Emma Peios/Alamy, (4) mediablitzimages(uk) Limited/Alamy.

Illustrator Credits
Dartmouth Publishing, Inc.

The National Geographic Society
John M. Fahey, Jr., President & Chief Executive Officer
Gilbert M. Grosvenor, Chairman of the Board

Copyright © 2011 The Hampton-Brown Company, Inc., a wholly owned subsidiary of the National Geographic Society, publishing under the imprints National Geographic School Publishing and Hampton-Brown.